BITCOIN CRYPTOCURRENCY FOR BEGINNERS

A NON-TECHNICAL GUIDE OF SMART MONEY STRATEGIES ON CRYPTO INVESTING FOR FINANCIAL FREEDOM

CONRAD PRESLEY

For permissions requests, speaking inquiries, and bulk order purchase options, email: publishing@uconcept.com.

ISBN: 978-1-960188-43-4| E-book

ISBN: 978-1-960188-44-1 | Paperback

ISBN: 978-1-960188-45-8 | Hardcover

Published by Unlimited Concepts, Coconut Creek, Florida.

www.publishing.uconcept.com

Book, Editing, and Cover Design by Janet M Garcia | UConceptDesigns.com

Published in the United States of America.

CONTENTS

INTRODUCTION

When the internet emerged in the late 1900s, only a few could have predicted how much it would transform our lives. It sounds pretty absurd but, can you believe that most people were reluctant to accept it and even dismissed it as a trend, for they just couldn't imagine how this strange and intangible network could ever become a part of their daily lives? Well, jokes on them because here we are, living in a world where the internet isn't just a part of daily life—it is THE daily life.

Today, we stand at a similar crossroads with cryptocurrencies. Contrary to the misunderstanding and skepticism that graced their early days, Bitcoin and its cousins are steadily proving their potential to revolutionize how the world thinks about finances. Right before our eyes, they have upgraded from just being "digital money" to now effortlessly challenging the traditional financial systems and institutions.

For centuries, we have been at the mercy of inflation, unstable exchange rates, and volatile financial markets. But like the famous knights in shining armor, the world of cryptocurrency is offering a decentralized alternative option that can make us almost immune to these real-world problems. This option also empowers individuals like you and me with a sense of control and other mind-blowing opportunities to reshape our financial future.

Now, before you start thinking this author got paid to do an ad for the Bitcoin brand, let me assure you that's not the case. I am living proof that anyone can create generational wealth and achieve financial freedom through crypto investing.

I began exploring Bitcoin out of curiosity and a desperate desire for financial independence. Like many of you, I was skeptical at first. Digital money that was completely outside the control of banks and the government? It was too good to be true and I struggled to believe it. Yet, as I eventually took that first step toward learning about cryptocurrencies, I began to see that my fears were baseless. Like a magnet drawn to its target, I read everything I could find about blockchain technology, the decentralized nature of cryptocurrencies, specifically Bitcoin, and its potential to provide financial freedom from inflation and market instability.

Things kept making sense as I continued reading and in no time, I found myself implementing my newly acquired knowledge and becoming a crypto investor! I do not wish to bore you with the details of my trajectories in Bitcoin investing. But let me make one thing clear: it changed my life and finances in ways I could never have dared to imagine!

As such, I couldn't help but wonder, "Do other people know about this life-changing financial formula?" The more I thought about it, the more I realized that many people, just like I had been, were either unaware or too hesitant to take a chance on cryptocurrencies. I imagined how they could benefit from the same knowledge and opportunities that had changed my life.

That imagination soon turned into a strong urge to share what I had learned. And as you can see, I gave in to that urge! This book you are holding in your hands is a manifestation of my dream to show you and many others that Bitcoin and other cryptocurrencies are reliable and effective avenues to become financially independent. So, whether you are a young adult, an entrepreneur, a corporate champion, or just someone who may not have a technical background but wants to explore the potential of this new financial catalyst, this book is your ultimate guide!

Across nine powerful chapters, you and I will explore the potential-filled spectrum of cryptocurrencies and how to invest wisely so that you can achieve financial freedom. Beyond just simplifying the dynamics of Bitcoin cryptocurrency, you will examine several step-by-step guides and effective strategies for short-term trading and long-term crypto investments.

Research shows that many people avoid crypto investing due to the perceived high risks involved. But let's be honest. Is there any financial venture that doesn't include risks? None! We simply have to learn to avoid them. Thus, this book will expose you to the common risk factors that often trip up crypto investors, especially in their early stages. More importantly, I'll show you how to avoid them using a robust risk management strategy tailored to safeguard your Bitcoin investments. This strategy comprises practical measures like understanding market trends, safety measures for knowing when to buy or sell, and even the due diligence required on your part.

Now, I understand that you may still have some underlying doubts about your decision to explore Bitcoin and crypto investing. You might be wondering if it's too late to invest, or if your lack of technical knowledge will affect your success rate.

First things first, I can assure you that it's never too late to start. Just look at top Bitcoin investors like Anthony Pompliano, who made his mark in his early 30s, or Michael Saylor, who embraced cryptocurrency in his 50s. They are the proof that successful crypto investing emerges from understanding and action, not age.

In the same way, I implore you not to worry about your lack of technical experience or knowledge. This book breaks down the complex concept of cryptocurrency into easy-to-digest sections that can quicken your understanding and help you become a pro at Bitcoin investing.

But while I have prepared this content to be straightforward and accessible for your learning needs, you must understand that it will challenge your pre-existing financial beliefs and stimulate your thinking. So, all I ask is that you be open-minded and actively engage with the material. Remember that success in any new venture requires a willingness to learn, adapt, and take action.

If you can efficiently demonstrate these qualities, I do not doubt that by the end of this book, you'll have amassed the knowledge and confidence needed to seize the opportunities that cryptocurrencies offer. I know you can do it!

So, turn the page, and let's unlock the potentials of Bitcoin and explore how you can maximize them to achieve financial freedom. Oh, I almost forgot to add... Welcome to the best era of your financial life!

UNDERSTANDING THE BASICS OF BITCOIN

In 2008, the Global Financial Crisis (GFC) hit the world and sent it into a financial meltdown only comparable to the Great Depression of the 1930s. The centralized banking institutions deemed "too big to fail" crumbled under their own weight and left "their loyal customers" to bear the brunt of their failures. These ordinary citizens were left helpless, homeless, and broke!

It is no surprise that they unanimously began to question and criticize the foundations of these traditional financial systems. Amid this crisis and uncertainty, a pseudonymous figure named **Satoshi Nakamoto** released a nine-page document that would eventually change the landscape of currency and finance. The document, titled "*Bitcoin: A Peer-to-Peer Electronic Cash System,*" proposed a novel concept that comprised a decentralized form of currency that could operate independently of any central authority. The release of that proposal marked the birth of Bitcoin!

THE BIRTH OF BITCOIN

If somebody has randomly told you this morning that Bitcoin emerged not just as a digital form of money, but as a symbol of rebellion against the status quo, how will you react? Most likely shocked and intrigued, right? Well, you are not alone!

With the exposure of the shortcomings and vulnerabilities within the institutions that had been the bedrock of the global economy for decades, Satoshi Nakamoto's release of the Bitcoin White Paper was revolutionary! In stark contrast to the centralized control that had proven unreliable, his proposal introduced the concept of decentralization which offered the grieving citizens greater control over their financial transactions and assets. It also promised them a secure and transparent way to conduct transactions free from the control of the institutions that betrayed their trust.

If you think about it a bit deeper, you will realize that Nakamoto's proposal gave the bereaved people an indirect opportunity to exert their revenge on their predators while still being on the winning side. How rebellious yet cool is that?

Well, you don't have to answer because the series of milestones that marked the early days of Bitcoin gives us an even clearer picture. These early milestones laid the foundation for the growth and rapid adoption of Bitcoin, that we now experience today.

The creation of the first Bitcoin block, known as the "Genesis Block," was one such integral achievement. It contained a hidden message that referenced a newspaper headline about bank bailouts and established Bitcoin's origin as a response to financial instability. Another incredible milestone was the first Bitcoin transaction which involved the purchase of two pizzas for 10,000 Bitcoins. This unusual transaction demonstrated the credibility and usability potential of Bitcoins as a medium of exchange, although a costly one by today's standards.

While the tales of these early milestones sound so cool, we must understand that Bitcoin's early journey was not without challenges. Although most people had lost faith in the banking system and were searching for a more reliable alternative, they had mixed initial reception to Nakamoto's idea, with many dismissing it as a fringe experiment like those in the early days of the Internet did. Due to this rampant skepticism and the fact that most people struggled to understand the concept and implications of a decentralized currency, the adoption of Bitcoin was very slow.

Yet, despite these hurdles, Bitcoin steadily gained traction and attracted a league of early adopters who believed in its transformative potential. This early development wouldn't have been possible without the passionate community of experts that formed around it. They included developers, enthusiasts, and visionaries, each of whom played a crucial role in shaping Bitcoin's trajectory.

These experts adopted online forums and mailing lists as their hubs of discussion and innovation, where they exchanged and debated ideas. Of all the discussion hubs, the *BitcoinTalk* forum emerged as a particularly significant platform, where these forerunners coordinated and celebrated many of Bitcoin's early milestones.

This community-driven approach, both concerning the early adopters and experts, was instrumental in refining Bitcoin's technology and expanding its reach. Without their collective efforts serving as the backbone, Bitcoin would never have gained the mainstream recognition it enjoys today!

SATOSHI NAKAMOTO AND THE GENESIS OF CRYPTOCURRENCIES

A puzzle even more intriguing than the creation of Bitcoin itself is the mysterious identity of Satoshi Nakamoto. Can you believe that the name doesn't even exist in reality? It is actually a pseudonym that could belong to an individual or a group whom no one has ever seen.

Besides adding a layer of allure and complexity to the story of Bitcoin, Satoshi Nakamoto's anonymity has sparked endless theories and speculations among the most brilliant minds across the globe. For more than a decade now, several research experts, journalists, and cryptocurrency enthusiasts have tried to uncover the identity of Satoshi but none brought forward a definitive answer. While some believe Satoshi to be a lone coding genius, others argue that it must be a team of experts, given the sophistication of the Bitcoin code.

Interestingly, some individuals have stepped forward to claim the mantle of Satoshi. However, none have provided the definitive proof needed to convince the skeptical Bitcoin community. So, instead of solving the mystery, these claims have only deepened the intrigue and turned Satoshi Nakamoto into a modern enigma.

But here is the plot twist you never saw coming: Satoshi Nakamoto wasn't always masked in this extreme mystery. Although no one can affirm what they look like or whether Satoshi is a single individual or a group, their presence was very real in Bitcoin's early days. Through emails and forum posts, Satoshi actively engaged with the budding Bitcoin community. They guided their discussions, refined the protocol, and ensured the network's stability.

After releasing the revolutionary Bitcoin white paper, Satoshi led the mining of the first Bitcoin set we earlier identified as *Genesis Block*. For two years, Satoshi distributed these Bitcoins to early adopters, like Hal Finney and Gavin Andresen with whom they communicated directly online. Other members of the early Bitcoin community also turned to them to ask questions, resolve technical challenges, and even receive software updates. In short, Satoshi spent two years creating a community, supportive and powerful enough to carry Bitcoin forward, independent of their involvement.

Sadly, they vanished in 2010 without leaving even a single clue. This sudden disappearance of Satoshi Nakamoto significantly impacted the Bitcoin community. Their absence meant that the revolutionary project had to continue without its original architect. Under normal circumstances, such abrupt leadership change will have dwarfed the prospects for any new technology. But the story was different with the Bitcoin team.

Satoshi's absence forced the community to step up, collaborate, and take ownership of the protocol's future. Developers from different parts of the work took the reins and fought hard to help Bitcoin remain an open-source project driven by collective input rather than a single visionary. As we said in the first section, their collective efforts and fighting spirit allowed Bitcoin to adapt and maintain its relevance in an ever-changing digital landscape. More importantly, they keep Satoshi's core principles of decentralization, transparency, and security.

Today, these principles, coupled with the success of Bitcoin, have inspired the development of alternative cryptocurrencies and blockchain applications over the years. Thus, we can safely conclude that despite their anonymity and mysterious disappearance, Satoshi's work will continue to influence how we think about value exchange and financial autonomy in the 21st century and for centuries to come! Isn't that a remarkable legacy?

DECODING BLOCKCHAIN: THE BACKBONE OF BITCOIN

Now that we have understood the mysterious yet fascinating history behind Bitcoin, it's time to focus on the invention itself. And there is no better place to start than its backbone!

Imagine a gigantic record book or ledger that meticulously keeps track of every financial transaction ever made. Now, instead of being a physical book sitting on a dusty shelf, picture it as a digital ledger that exists simultaneously on countless computers around the world. That picture you have is basically *the blockchain*, a decentralized technology that powers Bitcoin.

Unlike the traditional ledgers maintained by a central authority, blockchain operates through a network of computers that individually hold a complete copy of the ledger. This structure ensures that no single entity can alter the records without consensus from the network. In other words, it creates a transparent and tamper-resistant system.

Now, let's create a more vivid picture of what the blockchain ledger looks like in reality. It is composed of blocks that each contain a list of transactions and a unique digital fingerprint called a *hash*. This hash is a string of characters generated by a mathematical algorithm from the transaction data. Whenever you input data to initiate a Bitcoin transaction, the system uses the SHA-256 hashing algorithm, a one-way cryptographic function to transform your data into a block with a unique hash.

So, each block within the blockchain ledger comes with a special hash, which works like a digital signature to ensure the safety of the data. So, if anyone tries to modify your transaction data, the hash changes instantly and makes it clear that tampering has occurred.

You've heard the saying, "There's strength in unity," right? Well, blockchain technology takes that concept to heart. Each block references the hash of the previous block to create a secure and chronological chain of connection. This fascinating architecture, combined with the decentralized nature of the blockchain, forms the backbone of Bitcoin and makes it more secure than traditional financial systems.

However, no system is entirely immune to threats, and blockchain is no exception. A potential risk, known as a "*51% attack,*" could arise if a single entity were to control more than half of the network's computational power. Such extreme control could give them the ability to manipulate the ledger. But despite this risk, the sheer scale and distributed nature of the blockchain network make such an attack highly unlikely, especially as the network continues to grow. Isn't that good news?

Now, you might be wondering, "If the blockchain is this secure, how are users' transaction data added to its system?" In the blockchain, each transaction you make is broadcast across the network. Then, the gatekeepers of the Bitcoin network, known as *miners,* get to work. Their primary responsibility involves solving complex mathematical puzzles—a process described as *Proof of Work*— to validate each transaction you make before it's added to the blockchain.

In performing their tasks, miners group the transactions they receive into blocks and compete to solve these puzzles using their substantial computational power. The miner who successfully solves the puzzle first gets the privilege of adding the block to the blockchain. The other miners in the competition also get compensated with newly minted Bitcoin and the transaction fees from the transactions they've confirmed.

With this everybody-benefits reward system, miners become more motivated to invest in the necessary hardware and energy to keep the Bitcoin network robust and secure.

Once the winning miner adds a new block securely, changing it becomes almost impossible, as any alteration would require redoing the entire race from the start. This irreversibility ensures the security and integrity of the blockchain.

Although we have only examined the impressive potential of blockchain concerning Bitcoin, I must emphasize that its applications in the world today extend far beyond cryptocurrency. In supply chain management, for example, blockchain offers unmatched transparency and traceability with which companies ensure authenticity and ethical sourcing, and track their goods from the point of production to their final consumers. It is also transforming the dynamics of industries like food safety and luxury goods where the integrity of provenance is critical.

Do you also know that blockchain is the backbone of smart contracts, particularly on platforms like *Ethereum*? These self-executing contracts, with terms encoded directly into the system, automatically enforce and verify agreements without the need for intermediaries. It also minimizes the potential for disputes and fraud.

Based on our analysis thus far, you can agree that the potential of blockchain to revolutionize traditional systems is limitless with the promise of increased efficiency, security, and transparency across various sectors. So, as you consider these possibilities, think about how the continuous development of blockchain might impact the industries and services you interact with daily.

A BEGINNER'S GUIDE TO HOW BITCOIN TRANSACTIONS WORK

As a beginner, navigating Bitcoin transactions may seem intimidating at first. But trust me, it's simpler than it looks. Several aspects of a typical Bitcoin transaction replicate some of the familiar processes of traditional banking, although with a digital twist.

It all starts with creating a *Bitcoin address* or *public key*, which functions much like a bank account number. You can share with others so they can send you funds. A Bitcoin address usually comprises a string of alphanumeric characters generated by your *Bitcoin wallet*, which can be on your mobile, desktop, or any dedicated hardware device.

Once you have this address, you're ready to initiate a transaction whether to send or receive Bitcoin. To send Bitcoins, you must decide the amount of Bitcoin you wish to send, enter the recipient's address, and sign the transaction using your private key which is the secure and encrypted digital signature that proves you own the Bitcoin you're sending.

Your signature immediately generates a transaction message which gets broadcasted to the Bitcoin network. A relevant part of this message is the transaction fee, which is the small amount of Bitcoin that incentivizes miners to prioritize and confirm your transaction. Although these fees are minimal, they are necessary to maintain the efficiency and speed of the network that will process your transactions.

Once the winning miner successfully verified your transaction as legitimate, it gets recorded in the blockchain which is the confirmation that the Bitcoin you sent is now in the recipient's wallet.

Unlike traditional bank accounts, which display a direct balance, Bitcoin doesn't show an account balance. Instead, it uses *Unspent Transaction Outputs (UTXOs)* to track balances. So, it records your individual "*coins*" as Unspent Transaction Outputs (UTXOs) that can be spent in future transactions.

As such, when you receive Bitcoin, it's recorded as a UTXO in the blockchain. However, when you're ready to spend it, these UTXOs become inputs for your new transaction. To give you a more vivid understanding, you can think of UTXOs as the individual coins you use in reality. When making a transaction, you can combine them to add up to the amount you want to send, just like you'd use a mix of coins to make the exact payment at the store.

With these UTXOs, you are less likely to double-spend. It also makes your transactions traceable. To track the status of a transaction, you have to use a *blockchain explorer* which is a public tool that allows you to see the confirmation status and other relevant details of your transaction.

A popular example of a blockchain explorer is **Blockchain.com**. To use it, simply navigate to the site and enter your transaction ID in the provided search bar. The explorer will process the ID and display relevant details about that particular transaction, including the number of confirmations, transaction fees, and the associated inputs and outputs.

BITCOIN'S SUPPLY AND DEMAND DYNAMICS

Now, have you ever wondered why people in the crypto world value Bitcoin so much, even more than other cryptocurrencies? Well, it's simply because of Bitcoin's limited supply. There will only ever be 21 million Bitcoins. No more; no less! Like diamonds and gold, this in-built rarity of Bitcoins is what makes them valuable.

So, unlike regular money that governments and its central banks can print whenever they feel like it, Bitcoin's supply is fixed and baked into its code. No one can create extra Bitcoins out of thin air.

Now, do you remember we emphasized in the introduction that Bitcoin can protect you from critical financial problems like inflation? Well, this fixed supply is the main reason for Bitcoin's shield against inflation. According to economists, inflation occurs when more money is printed, which causes its value to decrease over time. But with Bitcoin, there's no printing press or central authority to make more. So, in short, its fixed supply ensures it cannot be devalued in the same way traditional money can.

To further increase its scarcity, Bitcoin holds something called "*halving events*" about every four years. During these halving events, the reward that miners get for creating new Bitcoin gets cut into halves, which slows down how quickly new Bitcoin enters circulation. Each halving event decreases the supply influx and makes Bitcoin even more scarce. So, if people's demand for Bitcoins remains constant or increases after such events, the value automatically rises.

However, several critical factors drive the demand for Bitcoin. One of the most influential is public perception, which is often shaped by the media. Positive news can spark excitement and lead to more people buying Bitcoin, while negative news can induce panic selling. How the media portrays Bitcoin—whether as a revolutionary financial asset or just a risky investment—has a big impact on its price.

Another significant factor is the growing involvement of big financial institutions in the Bitcoin market. As more banks and highly reputable companies start investing in Bitcoin, it gains more legitimacy and attracts more investors seeking stable returns and portfolio diversification. Ordinary citizens like you and I, see these Institutional investments as a vote of confidence. Hence, we become more willing to try the prospects and push the prices even higher.

Moreover, Bitcoin's use in everyday transactions is also expanding. More businesses, especially those with online stores are accepting Bitcoin. Some companies are even paying their international employees through Bitcoins. If we have more of these individuals and organizations using this digital asset, it will appeal to a wider audience and become integrated into our daily lives.

At this point, we have completed the first half of the groundwork for your exploration into smart Bitcoin crypto investing.

In this chapter, we have learned how Bitcoin and the general idea of cryptocurrency came about, the incredible technology that makes them work, and most importantly, their limitless potential to reshape and improve the world's financial system. It’s now time to learn about Bitcoins’ cousins and complete the second half of this crucial foundational puzzle!

NAVIGATING THE CRYPTOCURRENCY LANDSCAPE

One important lesson we took from the previous chapter is that the evolution of cryptocurrencies has sparked a revolution and challenged the traditional norms of money and value. Although Bitcoin takes center stage, it is but one player in the boundless and dynamic system of cryptocurrencies.

We refer to the wide range of cryptocurrencies that coexist alongside Bitcoin as *Altcoins,* which is a short-term for alternative coins. Developers from different parts of the world created these alternative coins to solve Bitcoin's limitations and explore new possibilities within the crypto world. These digital currencies bring diverse functionalities and address various needs, which add greater depth and complexity to the cryptocurrency ecosystem.

Take Ethereum, for example. You've probably heard of it—it's one of the most prominent Altcoins that stands out for its smart contract capabilities. Created by Vitalik Buterin and launched in 2015, Ethereum introduced a platform where developers could build decentralized applications (dApps). These applications run exactly as programmed, without downtime, fraud, or interference from third parties. This innovation elevated Ethereum beyond being just a cryptocurrency to become a decentralized computing platform. Hence, it is no surprise that Ethereum has enjoyed widespread adoption and impact, which has often made its market capitalization second only to Bitcoin.

Another powerful alternative cryptocurrency is Ripple (XRP), which has carved out a niche in cross-border payments. While Bitcoin focuses on peer-to-peer transactions, Ripple partners with financial institutions to provide fast and low-cost international payment solutions. This feature makes it attractive to banks and other financial services, though it has faced legal scrutiny from regulatory bodies like the SEC.

Then, we have Litecoin, which most crypto investors describe as the silver to Bitcoin's gold. This creation particularly boasts of quicker transaction times and a different hashing algorithm which aims to improve upon some of Bitcoin's perceived inefficiencies. Like Ethereum, Litecoin is also a popular choice for everyday transactions.

The market capacity and popularity of these highlighted Altcoins indicate their standing in the crypto world. While their adoption and usage rates vary, it is obvious that they collectively contribute to the diversification and expansion of the crypto market.

In the last chapter, we mentioned that Bitcoin relies on its miners' Proof of Work to validate transactions and add them to its blockchain network. While this process offers effective results, it's very energy-intensive. Many Altcoins, like Cardano and Solana, have tried to improve on this limitation by providing Proof of Stake (PoS), a more energy-efficient method where validators are chosen based on the number of coins they hold and are willing to "stake" as collateral. Hence, it not only reduces energy consumption but also democratizes the validation process.

Privacy-focused coins like Monero and Zcash offer another layer of differentiation by prioritizing user anonymity. These Altcoins employ advanced cryptographic techniques to overshadow transaction details and make them appealing to users seeking enhanced privacy.

Seeing these advanced features that Altcoins have over Bitcoin, you might start thinking, "Oh, maybe Bitcoin isn't that great!" Absolutely not! Bitcoin remains an integral part of any cryptocurrency portfolio.

Still, when you include Altcoins in your portfolio, they facilitate diversification. For crypto investors, diversification is a strategy to reduce risk by spreading investments across different assets. So, by including Altcoins in a cryptocurrency portfolio, you can protect your funds against the unpredictability of individual coins. Remember Altcoins often behave differently from Bitcoin and are influenced by distinct factors and market dynamics. As such, they can monitor performance trends and provide shields against market swings.

Above all, the inclusion of Altcoins in your cryptocurrency portfolio can potentially enhance its returns while reducing overall volatility. Thus, if you truly want to craft a balanced and resilient investment strategy, you must learn the unique attributes of Altcoins and their potential to complement Bitcoin.

THE EVOLUTION OF CRYPTOCURRENCY EXCHANGES

Cryptocurrency exchanges are platforms that allow people to buy, sell, and trade cryptocurrencies like Bitcoin, Ethereum, and other Altcoins we mentioned in the previous section. These exchanges act as the entry points to the crypto world. They also help users like you and me, maneuver different digital currencies.

Since their inception, cryptocurrency exchanges have experienced significant transformation by upgrading from simple peer-to-peer platforms to sophisticated centralized systems. In the early days, trading Bitcoin involved direct transactions between individuals often facilitated through online forums and chat rooms. These peer-to-peer exchanges were rudimentary and lacked the structure and security measures we see today.

But as the world's interest in cryptocurrencies grew, so did the need for more reliable and efficient trading environments. This increasing need led to the development of modern centralized exchanges like Binance and Coinbase, which offered more streamlined and secure trading experiences. These platforms provide users with relevant features, including the ability to trade different cryptocurrencies directly against one another, and traditional fiat currencies like the dollar and euro. This option for variety promotes liquidity and ensures that users can buy or sell assets without significant price slippage.

Many of the modern centralized cryptocurrency exchanges have also implemented advanced measures to protect user funds and data. Such measures include two-factor authentication, encryption protocols, and regular security audits.

Besides the high level of security, these platforms also feature intuitive user interfaces that make them accessible for beginners while providing advanced tools for experienced traders. However, you must understand that the fee structures differ across exchanges. While some charge a percentage of each cryptocurrency transaction, others implement a tiered system based on trading volume. As a trader, you must first figure out the cost system of any centralized cryptocurrency exchange you intend to use because these fees can impact your ultimate profitability.

Although centralized exchanges dominate the market today, decentralized exchanges (DEXs) are becoming more popular due to their offer of an alternative trading approach. Unlike their centralized counterparts, DEXs operate without a central authority and allow peer-to-peer transactions directly on the blockchain. With these features, DEXs eliminate the need for intermediaries, reduce the risk of hacking, and provide users with greater control over their funds.

A leading example is Uniswap, which has revolutionized the decentralized finance (DeFi) space by allowing users to trade tokens directly from their wallets. This innovation has made crypto trading more accessible worldwide.

Another critical difference between centralized exchanges and DEXs is that the latter mainly employ automated market maker (AMM) systems, which use algorithms to determine the price of assets based on supply and demand. With this advanced model, DEXs help in lowering users' transaction fees and increasing their privacy.

But despite advancements in both the centralized and decentralized types, cryptocurrency exchanges encounter different challenges and risks daily. One such problem is security. Exchanges are prime targets for hackers due to the large volumes of assets they hold. Over the years, there have been several high-profile breaches and such devastating incidents further emphasize the need for intense data security.

Nevertheless, modern cryptocurrency exchanges also struggle with increased scrutiny from regulators. Many countries require them to follow rules like Know Your Customer (KYC) and Anti-Money Laundering (AML) policies, which center on verifying users' identities and monitoring for illegal activities. Of course, we cannot deny that these regulations help safeguard consumers and prevent fraud. However, they can create operational difficulties for exchanges operating across multiple jurisdictions, particularly those operating internationally.

Ultimately, cryptocurrency exchanges must learn to tackle these challenges and remain adaptable to regulatory and technological changes. It is only by doing so that they can remain relevant and secure in this ever-evolving game.

INITIAL COIN OFFERINGS (ICOS)

So far, we have identified several enticing advantages of cryptocurrencies. But I promise you that there is so much more in store; one of which is that it offers you the chance to invest in the next big tech breakthrough before it even launches. Sounds too good to be true, right? Well, let's find out how it works.

In the cryptocurrency space, we have something called, "Initial Coin Offerings (ICOs)" which has become a popular method for founders to raise money for their projects. You can think of it as the crypto version of an Initial Public Offering (IPO) in the stock market.

But instead of selling shares like in an IPO, ICOs sell tokens, which can grant you, as a buyer, access to a platform, service, or even voting rights within a project. To acquire these tokens, you will most likely have to buy them using other established cryptocurrencies like Bitcoin or Ethereum which allow the startups to secure funding while directly engaging with potential investors and bypassing traditional banks and their strict regulations. Such an easy and flexible fundraising avenue, right?

Unsurprisingly, ICOs' decentralization of investment opportunities has captured the attention of entrepreneurs and opened doors for their small businesses to compete with the big players in the digital economy.

Nonetheless, launching an ICO is a high-stakes pursuit. The simple summary is that it starts an idea and evolves into a new token that gets introduced on the market. Now, what's the longer story?

The team in charge of the project first writes a "whitepaper," which is a document that explains the project's objectives, technology, and roadmap. It also serves as a pitch to prospective investors who want to know what the project promises to deliver.

Having created the whitepaper, the project team uses marketing campaigns to spread the word about the project, attract attention, and build trust. Once the project has gained sufficient interest, the ICO goes live and allows investors to purchase the project's tokens using the most popular cryptocurrencies.

After the ICO, the team releases the tokens to the investors. The distribution of these tokens is a critical moment, as it often coincides with the listing of the new cryptocurrency on exchanges. That coincidence provides liquidity and accessibility to a broader audience.

With the needed funds already raised, the team then shifts its focus to delivering on promises made in the whitepaper. To maintain their investors' confidence and guarantee the project's long-term success, the team must build a platform or service that the token represents.

As an investor, especially if you are still new to the game, ICOs can be tempting because they offer you the chance to get in early on a project that could skyrocket in value. Over the years, we have witnessed how countless early adopters of successful projects received incredible returns on their investments.

However, the risks are just as high. Since ICOs operate in a largely unregulated space, there are several stories of projects that failed or, worse, turned out to be scams designed to exploit unsuspecting investors.

Hence, you must exercise thorough due diligence and cautious optimism when considering an ICO investment. Take adequate time to measure the potential rewards against the risks and acknowledge that not all projects will succeed. Just as with cryptocurrency exchanges, caution should be your best friend in this unpredictable market.

The regulatory dynamics of ICOs is another major complexity. Regulatory bodies, such as the Securities and Exchange Commission (SEC) in the United States, monitor ICOs to ensure they comply with securities laws. The SEC applies the **Howey Test** to determine if an ICO qualifies as a security. If it does, the project must meet strict legal requirements, including registration and transparency.

Yet, this regulatory scrutiny is not unique to the U.S. Several governments worldwide are trying to figure out how to manage the challenges posed by ICOs. Although some countries have embraced this innovation and established clear regulatory guidelines to heighten the growth, others have imposed strict restrictions or outright bans. This conflicting regulatory environment can significantly affect the viability and attractiveness of ICOs. It can also influence how startup teams structure their projects and market them to potential investors.

But for you, as an investor, understanding these regulatory guidelines is non-negotiable. When you have adequate knowledge about them, you can easily tread carefully and stick to tokens with substantial returns on investment.

THE RISE OF NFT AND ITS RELATION TO BITCOIN

If you are already amazed at how ICOs open doors to early investments in promising projects, then brace yourself because like I said earlier, there is so much more! This time, we are focusing on Non-Fungible Tokens (NFTs), a revolutionary creation transforming how we can own and value digital assets.

Unlike Bitcoin or tokens from ICOs, which are interchangeable and serve as digital currencies or investment tools, NFTs are unique digital assets that represent ownership of specific items. It's just like owning exclusive things like a rare trading card, a signed album, a high-value piece of art, or even a signed autograph of your favorite celebrity, except it's all digital and verified on the blockchain.

Similar to how ICOs give startups a way to raise funds, NFTs offer creative individuals like artists, musicians, and game developers an opportunity to monetize their creativity globally without relying on traditional gatekeepers. So, let's say you decide to buy an NFT. What you will essentially get is the proof or rights of ownership for that unique digital item. Isn't that so cool?

Like Bitcoin and ICOs, blockchain technology provides the backbone for verifying and recording ownership of NFTs. It also heightens the transparency and security of each NFT, much like a certificate of authenticity in the art world.

Now, do you remember Ethereum, one of the most prominent Altcoins we identified in the previous chapter? Well, it has been at the forefront of the NFT revolution, largely due to its ERC-721 token standard. With this standard, Ethereum facilitates the development and trading of NFTs. It also leverages its smart contracts technology to enhance NFTs' appeal by automating royalties for creators whenever their NFTs get resold. This automated feature ensures that artists can keep earning from their work long after the initial sale.

If you're part of the creative world, I bet you're already imagining how you can use this innovation to build a lasting income stream and reach a global audience. I mean, why shouldn't you? NFTs have truly been the game-changer for many creators globally. Unsurprisingly, its growth has been explosive, with high-profile sales, like digital artworks auctioned for millions of dollars, spotlighting NFTs as a legitimate asset class.

As the market expands, more creatives and even organizations like gaming companies and art galleries are embracing NFTs to engage with their audiences in a more exciting yet secure way. This increase in market capitalization reaffirms NFT's potential as a new revenue stream for creators and direct methods of interaction with their fans.

OTHER TRENDS AND INNOVATIONS IN CRYPTO MARKETS

The growth of NFTs, as we have just seen, demonstrates the power of the crypto markets to empower individuals, specifically creators. But besides NFTs, the crypto markets have experienced the emergence of several trends and innovations that continue to extend their empowerment potential even further.

One such innovation is "Decentralized Finance (DeFi)", which seeks to offer its users financial services like lending, borrowing, and trading on blockchain platforms. So, instead of going to a bank and enduring the lengthy approval process, credit checks, and high interest rates, you can access these services directly and easily through the smart contracts of DeFi applications. Besides giving you what you seek, DeFi provides you with greater transparency and control over your assets. Think about it: with just an internet connection and notwithstanding your location, you can easily access these critical financial tools. Isn't that literally a gift?

Fortunately, the crypto market is the gift that keeps giving. Stablecoin is another top crypto innovation that can help you in your quest for financial freedom. Unlike popular cryptocurrencies like Bitcoin or Ethereum, which can experience significant price fluctuations, stablecoins aim to offer more stability. By pegging its value to stable assets or reserves like the US dollar, this innovation allows you to trade with stable prices which facilitates smooth transitions between your cryptocurrencies and traditional money. It also shields your cryptocurrency portfolio during unpredictable and difficult trading seasons.

Apart from stablecoins, central bank digital currencies (CBDCs) are also gaining momentum in the crypto market, as governments in countries like China, The Bahamas, and

Sweden are exploring digital versions of their national currencies. A CBDC is simply the digital form of a country's official money, issued and regulated by the government's central bank. So, you know how most cryptocurrencies, like Bitcoin, are decentralized and not backed by any central authority? In this case, it's the opposite. CBDCs seek to combine the benefits of digital currencies, like faster transactions and lower fees, with the trust and security of government oversight. In other words, CBDCs could make everyday financial transactions more efficient and accessible, while also providing more stability than cryptocurrencies. At this point, we have only a handful of countries developing and testing their CBDCs. However, as more countries join the party, these digital currencies could encourage wider adoption of blockchain technology and even change how we use money on a global scale.

Similar to how countries are testing CBDCs to make their financial transactions more stable and easier to use, institutional investment is also becoming an integral part of the cryptocurrency world, and bringing along trust and stability. Big investment groups, like hedge funds and asset management firms, are now putting money into digital currencies because they see the potential for high profits and a way to balance out their investments. This new wave of funds from industry leaders is helping to stabilize Bitcoin prices and making cryptocurrencies more credible in the financial world. In a few years when more experienced investors join the crypto space, economists estimate that they will bring advanced strategies and tools to make the market more stable and professional.

Beyond the emerging innovations and trends we have highlighted thus far, the future of cryptocurrency markets will likely be shaped by advancements in artificial intelligence (AI) and machine learning. These technologies have the power to process vast amounts of data at incredible speed. They can also uncover patterns and trends that human traders might likely miss. Thus, they are the perfect tool to automate our trading processes and make transactions faster, more efficient, and highly precise. That's a triple threat right there!

Ultimately, you must understand that there will always be emerging trends and innovations that reflect broader technological and economic shifts. Hence, it is best to stay informed about these trends and innovations as they evolve. With an increased understanding of these innovations, you are more than ready to embrace the gems of knowledge we will unravel in the next chapters of this book.

SETTING UP FOR BITCOIN INVESTING

Now that we have covered the basics of Bitcoin and other cryptocurrencies, it's time to start building your Bitcoin investment career. But before committing to the buying and selling process, you must secure two essential tools: the right Bitcoin wallet and a reliable cryptocurrency exchange.

Thus, in this chapter, you and I will analyze these tools in detail. You will learn about the different types of Bitcoin wallets, how to choose the one that matches your trading needs, and the steps to set it up securely. Then, we will make a final stop to show you how to select the most reliable cryptocurrency exchange. Trust me, by the end of this chapter, you will have all it takes to navigate the buying and selling process with confidence! Now, let's get started!

TYPES OF BITCOIN WALLETS

A Bitcoin wallet is simply a secure vault that safeguards your cryptocurrencies while providing you easy access when you need it. Like your physical wallets, Bitcoin wallets come in different types to satisfy various needs. They are mainly divided into two categories: hot wallets and cold wallets.

Hot wallets are connected to the internet which makes them fast and convenient for frequent transactions. So, if you need quick access to your Bitcoin funds, hot wallets are the perfect option! A beginner-friendly example of a hot wallet is Trust Wallet, which supports multiple cryptocurrencies and offers the convenience of managing your assets on the go.

On the opposite end, cold wallets are offline and prioritize security. They're your best bet for long-term storage and protecting your Bitcoin from online threats. Hardware wallets like Ledger and Trezor are great examples of cold wallets, as they offer strong security features to safeguard your private keys.

CHOOSING THE RIGHT WALLET

Now that you have understood the differences between the two wallet categories, the next step is to weigh your options based on some essential factors. Your primary focus should always be on security because you want a wallet that can effectively protect your assets from theft or loss. So, look for features like multi-signature support and strong encryption protocols.

After security comes the user interface which is especially significant if you're new to the crypto space. A wallet with an intuitive and user-friendly design can make managing your Bitcoin holdings much simpler. So, don't compromise it!

Reputation is another important consideration. Ensure that you only opt for wallets that have earned positive reviews and established a track record of reliability. For example, Coinbase Wallet is a popular and highly recommended wallet option for beginners. There are countless positive reviews about its user-friendly interface and two-factor authentication features.

Finally, your wallet choice must match your trading frequency and the types of cryptocurrencies you plan to store. If you are planning to stick to Bitcoin, then Coinbase Wallet can be your go-to option, as they specialize in storing and securing Bitcoin with simplicity and ease. However, if you seek to manage a diverse portfolio that includes Altcoins like Ethereum, Litecoin, or even newer tokens, Trust Wallet would be more suitable. As we said earlier, this hot wallet supports a wide range of cryptocurrencies and comes with features that allow easy management of multiple assets in one place.

SETTING UP YOUR WALLET

When you can select a wallet that fits perfectly with your needs as a crypto investor or trader, setting it up is a piece of cake. You begin by downloading and installing the wallet software from a trusted source. Notwithstanding the type of wallet you choose, you must consciously verify the authenticity of the source to avoid potential security risks. Remember security is a top priority in this game.

After installation, you will have to create a secure backup of your wallet data. Having secure backups of your wallet data ensures that you can recover your Bitcoin in case of device failure or loss. This backup is usually a set of recovery phrases or a seed phrase that serves as your lifeline or emergency code if you ever lose access to your wallet. So, be sure to save these phrases in safe and offline locations with zero chance of damage or theft. In case you missed it, the word, "location" is in plural form, as it is more effective to store your backups in multiple places.

Some newbie investors often make the mistake of creating digital backups. Please don't do that! Hackers tend to access such types of backups. So always do the offline version. You should also test the backup recovery process regularly to confirm that your backups are functional and that you can access your Bitcoin when needed.

Once you have that assurance, your wallet is ready to receive and manage Bitcoin, marking your official entry into the crypto investing world.

SECURING AND MANAGING YOUR WALLET

Creating a safe and offline backup is not enough to secure your now-installed wallet. It isn't a one-time task but rather a continuous responsibility that demands vigilance and awareness.

So after creating solid backups, always use strong, and unique passwords for your wallet accounts. You can enable encryption where possible, to add an extra layer of security.

You should also commit to updating your wallet software regularly. Developers, especially in the crypto space frequently release updates to rectify evident vulnerabilities of their applications and improve their functionality. So, try to stay current and update as quickly as possible to protect your assets from potential threats.

Securing your wallet also requires that you are cautious of scammers and deceptive websites that mimic legitimate wallet services. So, always double-check URLs and avoid clicking on suspicious links. Keep in mind that your vigilance is your best defense against unauthorized access and cyber threats. Here is a checklist to help ensure that you take the right steps to manage and secure your Bitcoin wallet for as long as possible.

SECURITY CHECKLIST FOR BITCOIN WALLET MANAGEMENT

1. Use a secure password manager to generate and store unique passwords for your wallet.
2. Enable two-factor authentication (2FA)
3. Regularly update your wallet software to benefit from the latest security patches.
4. Verify the authenticity of wallet software downloads and updates.
5. Store your recovery phrases safely and offline, away from digital devices.
6. Avoid using public Wi-Fi networks when accessing your wallet.

CHOOSING THE RIGHT CRYPTOCURRENCY EXCHANGE

With your Bitcoin wallet set up, your next mission is to pick a cryptocurrency exchange. This process is your ultimate foundational step to start your investment endeavors. Thus, your choice has to be reliable, secure, and appropriate for your needs. As in the case of your wallet, there are certain criteria you should consider to make the right choice. Let's find out what they are!

- **Regulation and Security Matters**

To succeed in Bitcoin investing, you must have an exchange that complies with regulatory standards and holds all the necessary licenses. This compliance isn't just about a bureaucratic necessity. More importantly, it's a way to protect yourself from fraud and legal complications. An exchange that adheres to regulations typically undergoes regular audits. As such, they have no choice but to maintain transparency with its operations.

The security records of your chosen cryptocurrency exchange are just as important as their legal compliance status. So, check out their security features too! Your best option is an exchange with advanced security protocols, like two-factor authentication and cold storage systems which ensures your assets get saved offline! These systems will protect your investments against hackers. With these measures present, you can be sure that your investments are safe against cyber-attacks and potential breaches.

- **Centralized vs. Decentralized Exchanges**

In the last chapter, we discussed the evolution of cryptocurrency exchanges and introduced the two main types: centralized and decentralized. When making your choice, you need to understand the key differences between them and how they match with your needs.

Centralized exchanges (CEXs) operate similarly to your regular financial institutions. They offer high liquidity and are quite easy to use. They also provide various tools to simplify your trading activities. However, they require you to entrust the platform with your assets, which can be risky in the event of a hack or internal mishandling.

On the opposite end, decentralized exchanges (DEXs) rely solely on blockchain technology. Due to the lack of intermediaries, these peer-to-peer systems allow you to trade directly with others and give you greater control over your assets. Although this autonomy reduces the risk of platform-related breaches, decentralized exchanges often have lower liquidity and may be more complex for beginners to navigate.

Ultimately, your choice should reflect your comfort level with technology and your priorities. If simplicity and a smoother user experience matter most to you, a CEX might be the way to go. However, if you are more interested in independence and greater control over your funds, a DEX could be an ideal choice!

- **Charge Fees**

Exchanges usually charge fees for trading and withdrawing funds. These fees can be a flat amount or a percentage of your trades. Although exchanges need this money to offer you the best services, they can eat into your profits especially if they are not accounted for, like those hidden fees some platforms tend to impose.

As a crypto investor, you can't afford to be caught off guard in that way. Your goal is to increase your profits and minimize costs as much as possible. So, when choosing your exchanges, you need to focus on those with transparent fee structures and discounts for high trading volumes. Ensure to read the fine print and go for what best benefits your pockets or Bitcoin wallet in this case!

CREATING AN ACCOUNT ON A CRYPTOCURRENCY EXCHANGE

After selecting an exchange that meets your criteria, you can proceed to the account creation page to sign up. Here, the system will ask for personal information to complete the Know Your Customer (KYC) requirements which help prevent illegal activities like money laundering and ensure the exchange operates within legal boundaries.

Once the system verifies your identity, you will immediately gain access to your account. Your first move should be to strengthen its security by setting up two-factor authentication which could require a code sent to your mobile device, whenever you log in or make significant transactions. This additional layer of protection not only secures your account but also heightens your peace of mind as you begin your trading activities.

In the end, the success of your Bitcoin investment pursuits begins with you selecting and setting up a wallet and cryptocurrency exchange that fits perfectly with your trading needs and personal priorities. By thoughtfully considering non-negotiable criteria like security, ease of use, and cost-effectiveness, you can confidently make the best choice for your success!

BUYING BITCOIN

Purchasing Bitcoin is a life-changing milestone for any beginner in the crypto world. Yet, I must admit that it can be extremely overwhelming. When I made my first ever purchase as a Bitcoin investor, I felt like I was preparing for the greatest exam of my life, rather than making a simple transaction like my mentor had suggested.

But let's be honest: there's nothing "simple" about buying Bitcoin, a digital asset as rare and valuable as gold. With a volcano of complex terms like "candle patterns," "market orders," and "price volatility" flying around, it's easy to become so confused and mentally exhausted. But fear not because I've got your back!

This chapter has been designed to simplify this critical process and to help you approach your first purchase with clarity and confidence. We will start by analyzing Bitcoin price charts and market trends to help you understand how to read the market like a pro. Then, we'll discuss how you can strategically time your purchase, to avoid being caught in the dangerous webs of emotional buying. After establishing these essentials, we will focus on the Bitcoin buying process, using a step-by-step template on how to do it right.

With this outline, you can tell that this chapter has a lot to offer. So, roll your sleeves and put on your crypto investing cap because you're about to make some big money moves!

BITCOIN PRICE CHARTS AND MARKET TRENDS

Despite having set up an appropriate Bitcoin wallet and cryptocurrency exchange, you cannot start buying and selling trading Bitcoins without understanding how its price moves and what trends can influence its value. Doing so will be like trying to drive a car in a new country without knowing the rules of the road.

Bitcoin operates in a market filled with dramatic fluctuations. Hence, you must master how to read and interpret price charts effectively. These charts serve as a visual representation of Bitcoin's historical price movement and give you valuable insights into how the coin might perform in the future.

Among the various chart types, candlestick charts are the most widely used. This chart not only shows the price range—open, high, low, and close—for a given period but also visually indicates market sentiment. A green candlestick indicates a price increase, while a red one signifies a decrease. Candlestick patterns, such as *doji, hammers, and engulfing patterns,* can signal potential market reversals or continuations which are valuable clues for you as an investor. If you can effectively analyze the pattern of these candlesticks, it becomes easier to determine market trends and make educated predictions about future Bitcoin price movements.

Apart from price charts, you also have to familiarize yourself with the concept of support and resistance levels. These levels are price points where Bitcoin tends to find a "floor" (support) or a "ceiling" (resistance). Recognizing these levels helps you predict price movements and plan the entry or exit points in your investment strategy.

Then, if you genuinely want to build a deeper understanding of Bitcoin's unpredictable pricing system, you need to invest in technical analysis. Technical analysis involves using various tools and indicators to interpret price data and forecast future movements based on historical data. Moving averages (MAs), the Relative Strength Index (RSI), and Bollinger Bands are just some of the tools available to help you assess the market. MAs smooth out Bitcoin price fluctuations to help you see the overall market trend while RSI measures the speed and change of price movements. It specifically tells you whether other traders have overbought or oversold a particular asset. Ultimately, when you master how to use these indicators, that understanding will surely give you the edge in reading price trends and making strategic decisions. So, get them if you can!

There are three major three types of market trends to Bitcoin's price. They include Uptrend (Bullish), Downtrend (Bearish), and Sideways (Consolidation). In an uptrend, Bitcoin's price consistently rises. So, you will most likely see higher highs and higher lows on the chart amidst this trend. However,

Bitcoin's price consistently falls in a downtrend which results in lower lows and lower highs. Finally, during the sideways or consolidation phase, the price stays within a defined range, though occasionally moving up and down within certain levels. So, it's neither bullish nor bearish.

Above all, you must always acknowledge that Bitcoin's price isn't just a random set of numbers but the interlinking of supply and demand, as well as other uncontrollable factors like market sentiment, news events, and broader economic issues. Hence, learning about its price movements at every slight opportunity is essential to becoming a successful investor.

TIMING YOUR BITCOIN PURCHASE

Once you have a basic understanding of Bitcoin's price movements and market behavior, it's time to focus on timing your purchase. Timing your Bitcoin purchase involves understanding market conditions and exercising patience. It can make all the difference in your investment strategy, especially given Bitcoin's volatile nature in which prices are capable of significant swings within short periods.

The most effective way to buy at the right time is to avoid emotional buying, particularly if it's driven by fear of missing out (FOMO). Of course, we know that the cryptocurrency market can be incredibly unpredictable. But as tempting as it is to invest in Bitcoins when prices are high due to a surge in media coverage or market hype, jumping in during a peak can lead to post-purchase dissonance or remorse if the price drops soon after.

So instead of relying on your emotional reactions to uncontrollable external factors, consider studying historical price data and monitoring market trends using the tools and materials we highlighted in the previous section. When you maximize these tools to keep your focus on long-term trends rather than short-term fluctuations, you will be in a better position to make strategic buying choices.

HOW TO BUY BITCOIN: A STEP-BY-STEP PROCESS

Having built a solid foundation of understanding the game rules, you are more than ready to purchase Bitcoin. Like I said at the beginning of this chapter, this process can seem intimidating. But if you stick to the steps we have highlighted so far in this chapter, and the ones we are about to examine, you will have Bitcoin in your wallet in no time and with your peace of mind completely intact. Now, let me show you how to play this game like a pro.

In the previous chapter, we already analyzed how to select and set up the right Bitcoin wallet and Cryptocurrency Exchange which are the first two critical steps of your first Bitcoin purchase. So, we'll move straight to step three which requires you to fund your chosen exchange account with fiat currency, such as dollars or euros.

To transfer funds directly to the account, you need to link your bank account or use a credit card. Some platforms like Coinbase, Bitget, and eToro, also accept PayPal, which offers more flexibility in your payment options. Nonetheless, each of these highlighted methods has its pros and cons. Bank transfers usually take lower charge fees but may take several days to process. Credit card payments, although instantaneous, often incur higher fees and interest rates. Then, we have the incredible convenience, although it is also subject to additional transaction costs. But don't merely consider the pros and cons of your chosen payment option. More importantly, you need to weigh these factors based on your preferences and the exchange's offerings.

Funding your account means you are ready to buy. So, you can choose between placing a market order or a limit order. A market order buys Bitcoin at the current market price and ensures a quick purchase. However, Bitcoin prices can fluctuate quickly, so you might have to pay slightly more than anticipated. A limit order, on the other opposite side, allows you to set a specific price at which you want to buy. In contrast to a market order, this approach provides more control over the purchase price but requires patience, as your order will only fill if the market reaches your desired price.

As in the case of your wallet and exchange selection, you must ensure that your choice of payment matches your priorities and investment strategy. Remember that the goal is to balance the immediacy of your transactions with cost efficiency.

After selecting your preferred order type and specifying the amount of Bitcoin you want to buy, your final step is to review all the details carefully and confirm your purchase. And voilà! You've successfully made your first Bitcoin purchase.

But hold up! Before you hit that confirm button, double-check everything to ensure there are no errors. Accuracy here is essential to avoiding costly mistakes!

While you may have completed your purchase, your Bitcoin investment still needs the utmost security. Of course, cryptocurrency exchanges offer convenience for buying and selling Bitcoins. However, they are not immune to hacking and other security threats. As we said in the preceding chapter, exchanges have been the targets of high-profile breaches in the past.

So, rather than leaving your Bitcoin on an exchange and exposing it to risk, you have to transfer it to a personal wallet for extra security. So, you see why we had to start this pursuit by selecting a Bitcoin wallet that aligns with your needs. With your Bitcoin wallet already established and having an enabled two-factor authentication, you can easily keep your account's private keys offline and out of reach from potential cyber threats.

Remember that you worked so hard to achieve that first Bitcoin purchase. You cannot afford to store it in an unsafe site. So, implement those crucial security measures and solidify the safety of your precious asset!

SMART MONEY STRATEGIES FOR BITCOIN INVESTMENT

Now that you've successfully navigated the process of purchasing Bitcoin, the next million-dollar question is: how can you maximize its potential to achieve financial freedom and create generational wealth? Your success as an investor lies in your ability to transform that initial purchase into a thriving investment.

To help you actualize that transformation, we will examine some smart money strategies that can make your Bitcoin investment work harder for you and maximize long-term returns. Let me tell you that these strategies are not only widely embraced but tested with impressive results to guarantee their effectiveness. So, brace yourselves because we are about to have a really powerful ride!

HODLING

I bet you raised an eyebrow at the spelling above, right? Well, no, it isn't a typo—at least not one I made on my own. HODLing has become one of the most popular investment strategies in the Bitcoin world, especially for those who believe in Bitcoin's long-term potential and are very patient!

But before we get into what this strategy entails and what it offers, let's address the elephant in the room. The term "HODL" actually started as a simple typographical error that quickly turned into a viral meme. Back in 2013, a BitcoinTalk forum user named GameKyuubi accidentally misspelled the word "hold" as "HODL" in a post advocating for urging investors to hold onto their Bitcoins even when prices fluctuate dramatically. Because his philosophy and investment strategy resonated with a lot of people, HODLing became its recognized name! What an unusual name origin, right?

Well, the best thing about HODLing is its simplicity. The strategy only demands that you buy Bitcoin and hold onto it for the long term with the belief that its value will certainly rise, over time. But does this belief hold water? Absolutely! Over the past decade, we have seen the value of Bitcoin rise from mere cents to thousands of dollars. Remember we explained in the first chapter that Bitcoin has an inherent limited supply and is designed to become even more scarce as the years pass. Due to these circumstances, you can be sure that implementing this strategy will increase the value of your digital asset and ultimately the size of your Bitcoin wallet.

Beyond the promise of growth, this strategy may also bless you with tax advantages. In many jurisdictions, holding assets for longer periods qualifies investors for reduced long-term capital gains taxes. That's a double killer, right there! You get to experience zero stress thanks to the minimal frequency of transactions and the absence of never-ending chaos in the short-term market. At the same time, you get to save on taxes! Wouldn't that be the perfect start to your crypto investment journey?

But before you settle for this strategy, you should know that HODLing is not for the faint-hearted. Bitcoin's inherent volatility can test even the most disciplined investors, so you must be ready to showcase incredible emotional resilience and patience. To help you better withstand market downturns and stay the course, you can choose to focus on the big picture which is that you can gain tenfold of what short-term investors are getting now, in the future. Recall that saying, the one who laughs last, laughs best—That should be your mantra!

DAY TRADING OR SWING TRADING

While HODLing is a long-term and passive investment strategy, day trading and swing trading are the go-to options if you prefer a more active role in your investment journey. The day trading strategy involves capitalizing on small price fluctuations by buying and selling Bitcoin within the same day. As you might have guessed, this speedy strategy demands your constant attention to market movements, quick decision-making, and the ability to react swiftly to changes. As a Day trader, you will often rely on minute-by-minute technical analysis, which, if you recall, we covered in detail in Chapter Three.

In contrast, swing trading offers a more laid-back approach that does not involve racing the clock! As an investor operating with this strategy, you will hold positions for several days or weeks while looking to profit from medium-term market trends. Just like the day trader, you will also use technical analysis, but with a broader focus on market trends and movements over time. Most importantly, you will enjoy freedom from the stress and time commitment required for day trading.

Nevertheless, we must emphasize that both strategies have their unique challenges and advantages. Day trading offers high potential returns but can be taxing, as it demands that you maintain composure and avoid impulsive decisions driven by emotions. Swing trading, while less time-intensive, still requires skillful analysis and an understanding of market timing. As a swing trader, you must be very vigilant because holding positions overnight can expose you to risks from unexpected market events.

In the end, if you are willing to choose any of the two strategies, you must consider three critical factors. The first is time availability. Day trading usually requires a full-time commitment due to its demanding nature, so it's most suitable if you can dedicate significant hours to watching the markets. In reverse, swing trading can accommodate your commitments with its flexible monitoring schedules.

Then comes your risk tolerance! Day trading provides substantial returns on the altar of increased risk and stress. So, if your risk tolerance is high, go for it! But if the reverse is your case, stick to the less-intense swing trading which has a moderate balance between risk and reward.

Finally, you have to match your financial goals with your chosen strategy to ensure that your efforts support your ultimate investment objectives. Don't settle but instead go for the option that will push you to achieve that which you seek.

DIVERSIFYING YOUR CRYPTOCURRENCY PORTFOLIO

Of course, Bitcoin is undoubtedly a valuable investment. But just as it is not advisable to put all your eggs in one basket, Bitcoin shouldn't be the sole focus of your portfolio if you are truly committed to achieving financial independence through crypto investing. Diversification is a powerful strategy that allows you to spread your investments across various assets. Can you recall that in chapter two we identified some highly valuable Altcoins? This strategy is your chance to maximize the potential of those alternative cryptocurrencies and complement Bitcoin's dominance.

With Altcoins like Ethereum and Litecoin offering smart contract capabilities and faster transaction speeds or Stablecoins providing stability amidst the volatility of cryptocurrencies, you can complement Bitcoin's performance and create a more resilient portfolio. A diversified crypto portfolio can protect you and your investments from the full impact of risky market downturns. For instance, if Bitcoin investment struggles at some point, the other cryptocurrencies will be there to keep you on steadier ground. In short, you become immune to the wild swings of any single cryptocurrency.

But before we get carried away by the powerful potentials of cryptocurrencies, I must establish that you can also diversify your portfolio using traditional assets like equities, bonds, and real estate, which can provide further stability and a shield against the high risk associated with cryptocurrency. Yet, you need to understand the correlation between Bitcoin and traditional markets to find the right balance for your investments. Without adequate knowledge, you could end up making the wrong choice.

In the same way, you should be careful not to exceed the borders of effective diversification. While diversification can be transformative for your investment pursuits, over-diversification can spread them too thin, and reduce your overall potential for returns. So, focus on quality assets that align with your goals and risk tolerance, when you are trying to diversify. Trust me, nobody knows you better than you! So, be honest with yourself and do things right!

OTHER RISK MANAGEMENT STRATEGIES

As I mentioned earlier, the crypto world is the gift that keeps on giving. Here's yet another example to back that claim! At this point, you've diversified your crypto portfolio, meaning you're not just focused on Bitcoin but have spread your investments across multiple assets. While diversification is a great start, it also amplifies the need to protect your portfolio from unexpected and unfavorable market trends. Luckily, the crypto space offers several effective risk management strategies that can help safeguard your investments. Let's analyze some of them.

- **Setting stop-loss orders**

Imagine if cars had emergency brakes that automatically kick in when they sense something bad is going on. Wouldn't that be a perfect way to reduce accident rates? Well, we may not have much in real life but the crypto world certainly offers them in the form of stop-loss orders.

These orders are designed to automatically sell a portion of your assets if their price falls to a predefined level. They take the emotional guesswork out of investing by ensuring that in the wake of falling market prices, your decisions will be driven by a strategy you defined yourself rather than panic. Most importantly, setting stop-loss orders will ensure that a sudden market drop won't leave you scrambling or completely deplete your holdings.

- **Position sizing**

This strategy involves determining how much of your total portfolio to allocate to each trade, based on your risk tolerance. By carefully deciding the size of each position, you can manage your exposure to any single asset, and prevent one bad trade from having a catastrophic impact on your overall portfolio. It's just like diversifying your bets in a card game to ensure that a single loss doesn't take you out of the game.

Now try to imagine what you will get if you effectively combine this strategy with stop-loss orders. Any ideas? It's pretty clear—you create a powerful defense against the unpredictable nature of the crypto market.

- **Hedging strategies**

Hedging is like adding armor to your portfolio to shield it further from adverse market movements. The two most popular hedging strategies in the crypto world are future contracts and option trading.

Future contracts allow you to lock in a specific price for your assets and create a safety net against price volatility. With futures, you're essentially betting against your holdings, and ensuring that even if the market turns against you, you have a backup plan!

With options on the other hand, you can purchase the rights, but not the obligation, to buy or sell an asset at a predetermined price. It gives you the flexibility to channel your strategy in response to market conditions without actually committing to a specific trade.

- **Regular portfolio reviews**

Just as you wouldn't drive a car without periodically checking the engine, you shouldn't manage a portfolio without regular assessments. This assessment involves analyzing your diverse investments to figure out your overperforming and underperforming assets.

With the findings from your assessment, you can then make informed decisions about whether to hold, sell, or diversify further based on current market conditions, your renewed investment goals, and risk tolerance. Perhaps, you may have to sell some underperforming assets to invest in undervalued ones. The rebalancing could also involve adjusting your exposure to different sectors based on economic forecasts. The decisions are yours to make. So, be intentional about getting it right!

- **Avoiding common mistakes**

Despite the powerful potentials of the four risk management strategies we have examined thus far, you must understand that they cannot be effective if you keep falling into the common problematic traps of the crypto space. One such trap is borrowing too much to invest in cryptocurrencies. Of course, the extra funds may increase your profits. But in the long run, they will magnify your debt and potentially leave you with debts far greater than your initial investment. So, avoid borrowing to invest as much as you can.

Then we have emotional trading where fear and greed can cloud your judgment and lead you to make impulsive investment decisions. The best way to avoid this costly mistake is to create a clear and rational plan that you can stick to, even when the odds are against you.

All in all, you should know that risk management is not just about protecting your investments. More than that, it's about empowering yourself to make confident, and informed decisions in the unpredictable crypto market. So, do your best to incorporate these risk management strategies into your investment plan and you will get to safeguard your assets while positioning yourself for long-term success.

LEVERAGING AUTOMATED TRADING TOOLS

In Chapter Two, we explored how Artificial Intelligence (AI) will likely shape the future of the cryptocurrency market. If you thought that the future was still years away, I have news for you—it's already here. In recent years, we have experienced an active transformation in how we trade, invest, and interact with our digital assets.

A prime example of this transformation is the rise of automated trading tools like trading bots, which have become essential for navigating the vigorous crypto markets. Trading bots are advanced algorithms designed to execute trades on behalf of users. These automated tools operate across multiple exchanges and make decisions based on predefined rules and market signals. So, they simply remove the emotional biases that tend to cloud human decision-making and execute investment strategies with precision and speed that you and I might find challenging to match. Yet, an even more compelling feature is that they work 24/7 and seize opportunities in a market that never sleeps.

There are various types of trading bots available today in the crypto space. They range from basic models that execute simple strategies to sophisticated AI-powered systems capable of learning and adapting to market trends in real-time.

While these highlighted benefits may sound quite fascinating, you should know that using these trade bots comes with risks. A trading bot's speed and efficiency, though advantageous, can lead to rapid mistakes if technical issues or bugs occur. Sudden and unexpected market shifts can also throw off even the smartest algorithms and cause them to make unintended trades that sometimes result in significant financial losses.

But notwithstanding these identified challenges, many traders strongly believe that the ability of these automated tools to stay objective and consistent far outweighs the downsides. Do you agree with them?

Well, experts in both the trading and AI fields have advised that we conduct intensive research and personal consideration before selecting the right trading bot, for doing so is the most effective way to limit their cons and maximize their pros. So, how do you find a bot best suited for your trading needs?

Start by evaluating the performance metrics of the bot options you are considering. These metrics should include success rates, returns on investment, and how the bot handles market volatility. If an option has a proven track record and positive reviews from other users, then it could be the one!

However, you also need your choice of bot to fit well with your personal trading strategy which comprises your risk tolerance, investment goals, and preferred trading style, whether it's aggressive or conservative. By getting a bot whose operations conform to your specific needs, you ensure that it acts as an extension of your strategy rather than a replacement. At the end of the day, you still get to be the one in charge!

And with that, we close the curtains on this chapter, where we explored over ten strategies to help you become a savvy crypto investor and a skilled risk manager. Now, you're not just equipped to make smart Bitcoin purchases, but you also know how to maximize their potential for financial growth. Whether it's through HODLing, trading, diversification, or automation, you've gained the tools to navigate the crypto market with confidence and ease.

So, you may ask, "What's next? Is there more to uncover on this journey to mastering crypto investing?" Absolutely! Turn to the next page and let's meet in the next chapter!

SECURING AND MANAGING YOUR PORTFOLIO

Seeing how often we have used the action words "secure" and "manage," in the preceding chapters, you can already tell that protecting your investments and staying organized are non-negotiable pillars of successful crypto investing. Although you now have the strategies to grow your Bitcoin and other crypto assets, you must work even harder to ensure that those hard-earned gains don't get snatched away by potential threats.

Whether it is cybercriminals hiding in the shadows or the ever-evolving regulatory environment, the crypto world has diverse risk factors that can block your achievement of financial freedom if not properly addressed. But worry not because like always, I've got your back.

Through the sections in this chapter, we will cover operational security practices that the most successful investors implement to lock down their portfolios like Fort Knox. We will also explore the legal landscape of cryptocurrency and its tax implications because trust me, nothing wipes out gains faster than penalties for non-compliance. So, without stalling any further, let's begin!

IMPLEMENTING OPERATIONAL SECURITY

The term, "Operational security or OpSec" encapsulates the essential security measures designed to shield your cryptocurrency portfolio and its holdings from potential threats. And it starts with your device!

As a crypto trader, you must have reliable antivirus and anti-malware software installed on the devices you use for accessing your cryptocurrency accounts. Such software helps to detect and eliminate harmful bugs within your devices that could compromise the safety of your investments. But beyond just installing this software, you must update them regularly to make them remain effective against the latest threats.

Then there is the network you utilize to access your cryptocurrency accounts. Public Wi-Fi networks, although convenient to use, are notoriously unsafe for financial transactions. The vulnerability of their data systems makes it very easy for hackers to intercept transactions and cause serious financial damage. As such, you must try your best to avoid.it when managing your Bitcoin and other digital assets. As an alternative, you can opt for a Virtual Private Network (VPN) to mask your IP address and heighten your online privacy. A VPN encrypts your internet connection and provides additional security that blocks your data from unauthorized access. So, you see, using a VPN doesn't only protect your crypto assets but also solidifies your overall online security!

In Chapter One, we identified that every Bitcoin account has two types of keys: the public and private keys. The public key is what you share with others to receive Bitcoin, much like an account number. However, the private key is the ultimate authorization code to unlock the cryptographic vault containing your Bitcoin. Hence, it has to be kept confidential, or else you risk unauthorized access to your funds.

Besides never sharing your private keys with anybody else—including your cute cats and dogs, one effective way to keep your private keys safe is to use paper wallets for offline storage. A paper wallet is a physical document containing your Bitcoin public and private keys, although it can be displayed as QR codes. Unlike digital storage, saving your private key offline enables you to cut off any chances of cyber criminals accessing it. They work online, right? So, if your private key isn't online, there is no way they can find it. But notwithstanding, you must make sure that you have the paper wallet kept in multiple physical locations with zero chance of damage or theft.

Now for your cryptocurrency exchange which allows you to set a personal password for logging into your account, the ultimate security tip is to ensure that the passwords are strong and unique enough to protect your exchange from unauthorized access. Remember you are the only one who gets to see it, so feel free to create the most random, incoherent, and weird-looking string of characters. But no matter the strength of your passwords, you must ensure to change it frequently. If you worry that these frequent changes could make you forget, consider using a password manager that helps you remember but still enhances the security.

THE IMPORTANCE OF TWO-FACTOR AUTHENTICATION

Even after you have created a strong password and ensured to update it regularly, your digital assets might still be a little susceptible to potent risks. However, two-factor authentication (2FA) comes in to provide the overall shield around your accounts. It's just like locking your house with a key and then adding a security code for extra safety.

Instead of relying solely on a password, 2FA requires you to add a second verification step which creates a combination of something you know (your password) with something you have (a code sent to your device).

The most common 2FA methods used in the crypto space are SMS codes and apps like Google Authenticator or Authy. While SMS-based 2FA is convenient, it's vulnerable to SIM-swapping attacks, where hackers intercept your messages. Authentication apps, on the other hand, generate time-sensitive codes and are more secure as they don't rely on your mobile network.

To enable 2FA on your cryptocurrency exchange, you simply have to access your account's security settings and select your preferred method. For apps, link them by scanning a QR code, and saving any backup code provided. Like your private keys, you must keep these codes in a secure and offline location as you need them to recover your account if you ever lose access to your device.

While we do not doubt that 2FA greatly enhances security, vulnerabilities like SIM-swapping or malware can still pose threats. But the good news is that you can solve the vulnerability by using a PIN with your mobile provider and keeping your devices updated with anti-malware tools to minimize risks.

RECOGNIZING AND AVOIDING COMMON SCAMS

The main job of 2FA is to handle the systems' role in securing your accounts. However, the ultimate responsibility of vigilance rests squarely on you. Scammers often sidestep even the best security systems by exploiting human error, eagerness, and naivety. Hence, fulfilling your due diligence is just as critical as the technology guarding your assets.

Among the most prevalent threats are phishing attacks, where fraudsters trick users into handing over sensitive information like private keys or login credentials by posing as trusted platforms. For example, you might receive an email urging you to update your account details using a link. The email usually contains a link to a website that looks almost identical to the real one. Yet, it's a trap designed to steal your credentials the moment you enter them. Always be wary of such unsolicited communications and double-check any links that request sensitive information. To recognize such scams, you can scrutinize the senders' addresses, check for spelling errors, and verify URLs before clicking.

Then we have the Ponzi schemes, which often promise high returns with little risk. These schemes entice investors by offering lucrative profits generated from the influx of new participants rather than actual business activities. The system eventually collapses when it becomes unsustainable and leaves later investors with significant losses.

To avoid such schemes, you must be skeptical of opportunities that guarantee unrealistic returns, especially those that require you to recruit others. If a project lacks a clear business model or refuses to disclose essential details, it's a red flag!

Scammers often exploit your fear of missing out (FOMO) to rush you into hasty investments. Please don't fall into their trap! It is also best to always research the team behind a project and ensure they have verifiable credentials and a legitimate track record. Anonymity might be acceptable in some contexts, but when it comes to handling your money, transparency is non-negotiable! You can also engage with community forums and discussion groups to gather diverse opinions and insights about new projects before you commit your money.

Being aware of these red flags can help you steer clear of potential scams. However, if you suspect that you've encountered a scam, it's crucial to act swiftly. Report the fraudulent activity to relevant authorities, such as the Federal Trade Commission (FTC) or the Commodity Futures Trading Commission (CFTC) in the United States. Many countries have specific agencies dedicated to handling cybercrime and fraud.

You can also contact your exchange or wallet provider immediately if you notice unauthorized transactions. They may have protocols in place to freeze your account and prevent further losses. Being proactive and vigilant can minimize the impact of a scam on your assets. So, ensure to document all communications and transactions related to the scam, as this information can be valuable in any investigation or recovery effort.

The impact of falling for cryptocurrency scams can be nothing short of catastrophic, as we saw in the infamous 2014 Mt. Gox hack. At its peak, Mt. Gox was the largest Bitcoin exchange in the world and handled around 70% of global Bitcoin transactions. But after a massive security breach, the platform lost 850,000 Bitcoins which is worth hundreds of millions of dollars. This loss led to its dramatic collapse and eventual bankruptcy.

Although this incident happened over ten years ago, its shockwaves still ripple through the crypto community today and serve as a harsh reminder of why it's necessary to choose secure and trustworthy platforms. Notwithstanding, we keep seeing a surge in initial coin offering (ICO) scams, where fraudulent projects have raised millions, only to disappear without a trace and leave investors high and dry.

These traumatic cases are a wake-up call that reinforces the need for diligence and skepticism. So, as you prepare to step into the crypto space, acknowledge that it's not just about seizing opportunities but also about thoroughly vetting them.

Never take the plunge on any project without verifying its sources and transparency.

UNDERSTANDING THE LEGAL LANDSCAPE

At the beginning of this chapter, I emphasized that nothing wipes out your gains faster than penalties for non-compliance. This statement is especially true when it comes to Bitcoin investing.

The global regulations around cryptocurrency are a mixed bag, with each country setting its own standards. Some places, like El Salvador, have fully embraced Bitcoin and even recognized it as legal tender, But others, like China, have imposed bans on cryptocurrency transactions to maintain financial stability and governmental control.

These critical differences can create confusion and uncertainty for investors, especially beginners. Clear regulations often bring stability and make it easier to navigate the market. However, unclear or overly restrictive laws like in China, can lead to hesitation and risk.

To stay on the right side of the law, you need to understand and follow important compliance measures like Anti-Money Laundering (AML) and Know Your Customer (KYC) regulations, which require you to verify your identity and ensure your transactions are legitimate. These bureaucratic processes aren't just to protect the financial system, but also to save you from legal trouble.

Apart from El Salvador and China, many countries also have reporting requirements for large transactions like crypto trading. Ignoring these rules could lead to fines or even criminal charges that can erase your hard-earned gains in an instant. So, take some time to learn about the legal trading requirements in your jurisdiction and do the right thing!

Let's also not forget that these regulations are always changing. Remember we mentioned that central banks are now testing and developing digital currencies called CBDCs. Although we are yet to know how they will operate, we are quite certain that this new development will shape how cryptocurrencies like Bitcoin get treated in the future. They could either work alongside Bitcoin or compete with it, depending on how they're regulated.

So, how do you stay ahead of these developments? Keep an eye on cryptocurrency news from trusted sites like CoinTelegraph or CoinDesk. And if you're unsure about your legal responsibilities, don't hesitate to consult a legal expert who knows the ins and outs of crypto regulations. By staying informed and compliant, you will not only protect your investments but also increase your confidence in scaling through unpredictable legal regulations.

PREPARING FOR TAX IMPLICATIONS

As we've just explored in the previous section, understanding the legal landscape is critical to building a successful crypto investing career. But beyond adhering to regulations, compliance extends to how you handle the tax implications of your investments.

Trust me, nobody including me likes doing taxes. But you know what? You cannot afford to ignore them because doing so can cost you dearly. Failing to understand the tax treatment of Bitcoin can lead to penalties that wipe out your gains just as quickly as non-compliance with broader legal requirements. Since you wouldn't want that, let's break down what you need to know to stay on top of your tax obligations and keep more of what you've earned.

In terms of taxes, Bitcoin and its Altcoin cousins are often classified as an asset or property rather than a currency. This statement implies that your transactions—whether you're selling them, trading them for other cryptocurrencies, or even using them to buy goods—may be subject to capital gains tax.

So, let's say, you sell Bitcoin for more than you paid. You have made a profit, right? That's a "capital gain," and that gain is taxable! However, the amount you owe the state depends on how long you hold the Bitcoin. If it's less than a year, you will likely pay a higher short-term capital gains rate. However, when you have held it longer, you may qualify for a reduced long-term rate, which is a financial silver lining. Doesn't that sound familiar? Yes, The HODLing Strategy! Here is how it works!

But that being said, you should know that tax rules vary widely depending on where you live. Some countries, like Germany, offer tax exemptions for cryptocurrencies held longer than a year, while others impose stricter policies. For this reason, you must be intentional about understanding your local tax laws. This knowledge will not only ensure your compliance but also show you how to optimize your strategy to keep as much of your hard-earned gains as possible.

In addition to learning about your local tax laws, you can also build the habit of meticulous record-keeping to save your sanity (and your wallet). Although it might sound tedious, having accurate records of every crypto transaction you make is a game-changer. They help you calculate capital gains, track losses, and ensure you don't miss any taxable events—like when you use Bitcoin to buy something.

Of course, you don't have to create these records manually. There is a crypto tax software that you can install on your device and link to your accounts to track every one of your trades and generate reports automatically. Yet, it is also necessary to have personal copies of receipts, transaction confirmations, and anything else that proves your cost basis, so that if the taxman ever comes knocking, these records will protect you from penalties and fines.

Despite taking these intentional compliance approaches, you must know that steering crypto taxes isn't always straightforward. Every crypto trader is susceptible to making mistakes like underreporting gains or forgetting to report taxable events like swapping Bitcoin for Ethereum. Such mistakes can lead to audits and hefty penalties. So, to prevent their occurrence, you can consider working with a tax professional who is already familiar with crypto regulations. Such a person can ensure your reporting is accurate and compliant. In short, they can save you from unnecessary headaches.

Based on what we have explored in this chapter, can you see now that buying and trading cryptocurrencies is just the tip of the iceberg when it comes to investing in crypto? The bigger game lies in how well you can protect and manage what you are working so hard to build. So, strive to be that Bitcoin investor who sets up operational security measures, stays sharp to avoid scams, and keeps an eye on the ever-changing legal and taxation laws. If you can be that person, you will certainly get to hold onto your assets and secure your financial freedom!

OVERCOMING COMMON CHALLENGES IN BITCOIN INVESTING

I bet you saw this chapter title and thought to yourself, *"Wait a second! Haven't we been tackling challenges since Chapter 3?"* And honestly, you'd be right! Bitcoin investing throws its fair share of complexities at you from the get-go. Yet, I must emphasize that most of the challenges we have highlighted so far are more on the technical side.

However, in this chapter, we're moving into a different territory which comprises the emotional, and psychological hurdles you will likely encounter after taking your first steps into Bitcoin investing. Because let's be real; profitable investments are not based on only numbers and strategies. You will need emotional resilience to weather unfavorable market fluctuations, confidence in the face of skepticism, and decision-making skills that keep you from second-guessing yourself into paralysis.

These concepts might sound abstract, but trust me, they can make or break your crypto journey. So, let's get into it!

THE EMOTIONAL APPROACH TO DEALING WITH MARKET VOLATILITY

Ask any crypto trader, especially those in their early years, and they'll tell you about the gut-wrenching anxiety that creeps in when prices tumble unexpectedly. In such critical moments, you will likely feel a knot in your stomach with immense fear urging you to cut your losses and sell off your digital assets. But in reverse, when the market rates are bullish and rising, the euphoria it creates can make you feel invincible and tempted to invest beyond your means.

Of course, we know that these emotional highs and lows are normal and human. But they can cloud your judgment and lead to impulsive decisions that destroy your long-term goals.

So, how do you regulate this extreme emotional rollercoaster to ensure they don't become your nemesis? One word—mindfulness! Engaging in mindfulness practices —like meditation, journaling, working out and even just sitting in silence for a while— allows you to take a step and clear your mind of its stressful chaos. When you have increased clarity, it's easier to make rational decisions rather than reacting to highly stimulated emotions like fear and greed.

You can also create well-defined trading plans beforehand to set clear rules for your buying and selling activities. These predefined plans remove the guesswork and reduce the risk of making decisions based on impulse. They act as a compass that provides you with a sense of control when everything else feels unpredictable.

Perhaps the most critical strategy is maintaining a long-term perspective that focuses on broader investment goals rather than short-term fluctuations. Yes, we are referring back to the HODLing investment strategy! So, consider implementing this strategy while being mindful that the cryptocurrency market has weathered several storms and consistently shown resilience over time. But you don't have to take my word for it, you can go through historical data on the subject. You will surely find past downturns, which were often followed by mind-blowing recoveries.

Beyond its financial rewards that we highlighted in Chapter Five, holding on to your investments and ignoring the noise of the volatile crypto market, increase your emotional resilience as an investor. With this resilience, you can cruise through the unpredictable waters of Bitcoin investing with greater clarity and your emotions fully in check!

AVOIDING ANALYSIS PARALYSIS AND MAKING INFORMED DECISIONS

As a beginner in Bitcoin investing, you can easily get stuck in analysis paralysis where every option seems risky and you get bombarded with the sheer volume of information. Rather than appreciate the diversity, you become frozen by the fear of making the wrong choice. As such, you spend so much time weighing your options. Eventually, you don't take any steps until the market shifts and the game-changing opportunities slip away from your fingers.

Sounds frustrating, doesn't it? Well, the harsh reality is that even experienced traders like me aren't immune to analysis paralysis now and then. But fortunately for you, it is not inevitable and with the right approach, you can avoid it.

The ultimate key to avoiding analysis paralysis is to simplify your decision-making process and trust your strategy. So, start by setting clear investment goals that fit well with your financial objectives and risk tolerance. With these goals acting as a guide, you can filter out distractions and focus only on what truly matters.

Another effective simplification strategy is to limit your sources of information. In the digital age, you get bombarded with news, opinions, and analyses from countless channels which leads to information overload. So, stick to a few trusted sources and indicators that fit your strategy. By narrowing your focus in this way, you can cut through the noise and make more confident decisions.

This limiting strategy can also extend to your market analysis metrics and technical indicators. In Chapter Four, we examined several of these indicators ranging from Moving Averages (MAs), and the Relative Strength Index (RSI), to Bollinger Bands and market sentiments. Although you have this wide variety, it is best to choose indicators that are relevant to your investment strategy. Doing so helps to enhance your focus and clarity. More importantly, the presence of fewer options makes you less prone to analysis paralysis.

Now, does the term "over-diversification" sound familiar? Of course, we mentioned it in the finale of Chapter Five as something to be cautious about, as you seek to add more digital assets to your portfolio. Beyond diluting your returns, over-diversification adds unnecessary complexity to your strategy and can trigger analysis paralysis. So, avoid it and strive to create a balance between diversifying your investment portfolio and keeping it manageable.

All in all, you must learn to take action, even if it's a small step. No investment decision is perfect, but doing nothing is often worse than making a mistake you can learn from. No one becomes an expert overnight. It takes time and experience to develop a sense of what works for you. But I promise you, when that growth begins to happen, you will find it easier to trust your instincts and take decisive actions even in the face of risk.

FINDING CREDIBLE SOURCES OF CRYPTOCURRENCY INFORMATION

In the same way that a sailor needs a compass to navigate the angry sea during a storm, you must have access to reliable information to cruise through the unpredictable lanes of Bitcoin investing. Building profitable investment demands not just any data but data that you can trust.

Unfortunately, misinformation and fake news are available in their multitude, ready to mislead and potentially cost you financially. Now more than ever, it is so easy to find news headlines or poorly researched articles that incite panic and force traders to make hasty decisions that simply destroy their investment strategy. But when it comes to accurate information that can empower you to make informed choices and anticipate market shifts with greater confidence, it's almost like finding a needle in the sand.

Thus, you need a discerning eye and mind to differentiate credible information sources from the chaotic clutter. So, every time you come across information about Bitcoin or its Altcoin cousins or the crypto market in general, your first move should be to evaluate the expertise of the author. Ensure that the writer has established themselves as knowledgeable in that field. So, they should be a seasoned investor or respected analyst whose background demonstrates a track record of insightful and accurate analyses.

After verifying the credibility of the author, cross-reference the information across multiple sources. If several reputable outlets confirm the same data or trend, it's more likely to be accurate. But if not, the information isn't likely true/ By taking time to complete this triangulation process, you can filter out the chaotic noise and ascertain that you are basing your investment decisions on facts rather than speculation.

If you are in search of credible platforms for your regular cryptocurrency updates, you can check out CoinDesk and CoinTelegraph. These sites are highly regarded in the crypto space for delivering timely news and analysis, crafted by industry experts who understand both the basics and critical details of the digital currency landscape. They can keep you informed on everything from regulatory changes to technological advancements, which provides a solid foundation for your investment decisions.

You can also consult popular blockchain explorers which offer a wealth of transaction data that enable you to verify the flow of assets and gain insights into market dynamics. These explorers are also effective tools for tracking the movement of Bitcoin and other cryptocurrencies. So, if you genuinely want a clearer picture of the market's pulse, they are your go-to options.

Then we have community forums and online groups which can be goldmines of information, especially when moderated by experienced individuals who can drive discussions in productive directions. The diverse perspectives you will find there can broaden your understanding and introduce you to innovative ideas. Yet, you must be cautious when participating. Sometimes, these forums post anonymous advice that can lead you astray. You might also discover that the herd mentality sometimes tries to overshadow your rational thinking. But rather than following the crowd blindly, you should balance community insights with personal research and judgment.

Of course, there is no way we can talk about credible sources of information without highlighting the internet. But while this magnanimous network has so much information to offer, not all of it is beneficial. As such, you must maintain a skeptical mindset and question the validity of every internet source and the motivations behind it. Sometimes, the most valuable insights come from those who have no vested interest in influencing the market but are simply passionate about sharing knowledge. So, be sure to find and engage with such individuals, whether through their interviews, podcasts, or blogs! Trust me, drawing snippets of their knowledge can add great depth to your understanding of Bitcoin and its many complexities.

Ultimately, finding credible crypto information sources demands that you remain vigilant and continuously refine your ability to filter out the unreliable while embracing the trustworthy. As you improve this skill, you will realize that it not only enhances your investment decisions but also builds your confidence as a participant in the cryptocurrency world. Like a champion, you will be ready to face its challenges and opportunities head-on.

HANDLING SKEPTICISM AND BUILDING CONFIDENCE

Remember that initial skepticism you felt toward cryptocurrency when you first learned about it? The harsh truth is that your reaction is not unfounded and to be honest, it never really goes away even as you grow as an investor. Within the crypto world, there are a multitude of factors that keep shaking the confidence of many potential investors and planting seeds of doubt in the minds of the active ones.

One such factor is high-profile hacks like the Mt. Gox exchange collapse which exposed the vulnerabilities of the crypto world and increased the fear for the safety of our digital assets. Then we have another layer of complexity in the form of ever-changing regulations and governments worldwide who still seem to be figuring out how to handle cryptocurrencies. Because we have no certainty as to what these authorities would say or do next, both new and veteran investors remain confused and concerned about potential legal repercussions. Finally, there is the media who never stop oscillating between portraying Bitcoin as a revolutionary asset and a speculative bubble. Their inconsistency continues to amplify the fear of innocent investors and leave us unsure of whom to trust.

Although we cannot be blamed for our human reactions to these prevailing conditions, we must learn to overcome our skepticism so that we can focus on maximizing the potential of Bitcoin investing for our financial growth. Hear me out; you cannot build confidence as an investor or enjoy the positive side of this game if you have your head constantly buried in the negative.

You must learn how to silence that skeptical voice in your head when the need arises and the best way to start is educating yourself. When you intentionally focus on consuming reliable resources like books, online courses, and webinars, this educational content will clarify the dilemmas you have about Bitcoin and crypto investing, that may be fueling your skepticism more than usual. They will also allow you to see its potential benefits, even those you have no idea existed.

The truth about life is that bad news sells faster than good news. Thus, the uncertain and risky details about Bitcoins and Altcoins are all over the place. But when it comes to the good and life-changing parts, we barely see a quarter of them. I bet that you've had so many positive ah-ah moments since you started reading this book. Such is the power of knowledge! When you have more understanding of this game, you may not trust it completely. However, you will build confidence and trust in your ability to navigate its ups and downs.

Besides seeking knowledge through educational resources, you can also connect with experienced investors to overcome your skepticism and become more confident. By seeking the mentorship of such individuals, you get to draw valuable insights from their firsthand experiences. They may help you dispel myths, and provide guidance.

But your circle should not only accommodate veteran investors. You can build a network of crypto-investing peers who are willing to share their resources and knowledge as much as you are. Being with them will enable you to experience a sense of community and reduce the feelings of isolation and uncertainty.

Finally, you must have realistic expectations to transform your doubts into informed convictions! By now, you should have understood that the crypto world is far from a fairytale and the potential for gains comes hand-in-hand with the possibility of losses. So, embrace that long-term growth. Some crypto traders actually become more skeptical and doubtful of their investment decisions not because of the game itself. Rather, their skepticism is born out of their failed attempt to chase overnight riches. They become traumatized by the financial damages from Ponzi schemes and blame it on the volatility of the crypto markets.

Please don't be that person. Stick to the rules of the game! Set incremental milestones to track your progress and celebrate the small victories that come along the way. Trust me, those desired successes will come gradually and the more they emerge, the more you become confident and committed to your investment strategy.

In all four sections of this chapter, one message stands out and it is that successful investing isn't about being perfect but staying adaptable and learning from each step of your journey. So, whether you're working to build emotional resilience, avoid the trap of analysis paralysis, or overcome lingering skepticism, strive for progress, and not perfection. If you can embrace the process and keep moving forward, your success in Bitcoin investing is truly guaranteed! I promise you!

BUILDING YOUR BITCOIN SUPPORT SYSTEM AND PERSONAL GROWTH

The wise historian, George Burton Adams once said, *"There's no such thing as a self-made man."* This truth rings especially clear for Bitcoin investing. Of course, you might feel like you're flying solo while watching the market or making big investment moves from your laptop at 3 a.m. However, the ultimate reality is that you need both internal and external support to stay the course and successfully achieve financial freedom. Whether it is trading mates to bounce ideas off of, mentors to guide you, or a mindset that keeps you cool when things get wild, a well-rounded support system can make all the difference in your success story.

Thus, our goal in this chapter is to examine how to surround yourself with the right people, learn from the best, and develop a mindset that helps you roll with the ups and downs of Bitcoin investing. We will also uncover tips for keeping your life in balance because let's be real, Bitcoin investing is just one part of the bigger picture.

So, let's dig in and start building the support system that'll set you up for success!

NETWORKING AND CREATING MEANINGFUL CONNECTIONS

Due to the valuable nature of Bitcoins, people from outside often regard its community as an exclusive place where you need huge amounts in your accounts to get in. As a beginner, it is so easy to have this mentality as well. However, it's pretty false. In reality, the Bitcoin community is a lively and growing space filled with people who are just as curious, excited, and sometimes as confused as you are. It is where investors, tech enthusiasts, and innovators come together to swap stories, share ideas, and figure out what's next for Bitcoin.

Trust me, you do not need a secret handshake or VIP access card to get in! If you want to join and make meaningful connections in this space, you've just got to show up at the right places. Bitcoin meetups within your local areas and global cryptocurrency conferences are great places to start.

Unlike the common tech-based gatherings, these events go beyond just sitting through presentations. They're buzzing with infectious energy and impactful conversations that supply knowledge that you may never find in traditional textbooks. Most importantly, these gatherings are your best opportunities to meet other traders—at the same or higher levels than you—with whom you can forge partnerships and gain exposure to the most lucrative opportunities in Bitcoin investing. Even better, you may connect with folks who will later become your best buddies. Just like that, you start creating a support system! And it's not just any random person, but individuals who understand your circumstances and can relate personally when you are ranting about market fluctuations or losses. They know the right things to say at the right time to make you feel much better.

Beyond just participating in these conferences and meetups, you can take things a notch and try volunteering. Doing so will get you to work alongside industry insiders while soaking up all the expert-led educational sessions firsthand. It also gets you a front-row seat to the magic happening.

However, if you are unable to attend the physical events, there are online alternatives like forums and discussion groups. These platforms offer you and other investors from around the world a space to ask questions, share insights, and discuss trends. While they may not be as energetic and intimate as the physical ones, these online spaces allow you to learn and network with like-minded individuals from the comfort of your home.

Apart from forums, social media platforms like Twitter and LinkedIn are equally powerful tools for connecting with thought leaders and staying updated on industry developments. So, take a chance on them and network!

Yet, you must understand that networking extends more than exchanging business cards or expanding your contact list. It's more about following up and nurturing the relationships you start. So, if someone shares valuable insights with you at an event, don't let the connection fade away. Instead, send a thoughtful message afterward and thank them for their time. Also, let them know you'd love to keep the conversation going. Whether you're looking for a mentor, an accountability partner, or someone to collaborate with, that simple text could ignite a meaningful partnership.

So, don't hold back but instead put yourself out there and join the conversation. In no time, you will see your non-existent network growing into a strong support system that uplifts every aspect of your investment journey.

MENTORSHIP AND LEARNING FROM SUCCESSFUL BITCOIN INVESTORS

In building a strong support system, few things are as valuable as having a mentor by your side. A mentor, in this context, is someone who has lived, survived, and conquered the wild twists and turns of Bitcoin investing. They've earned their wisdom through experience, and they can guide you through the inevitable highs and lows of your journey. A good mentor can also save you from countless mistakes, point you toward smarter strategies, and help you approach your goals with clarity and confidence. In short, they can be your anchor in this unpredictable game.

Finding a mentor may seem intimidating at first, but it's often simpler than you think, especially in the crypto world. Remember the practical networking tips from the previous section? You can use those to not only find trading buddies but also connect with experienced investors willing to mentor you. Whether it's by exchanging contacts or volunteering at events to gain closer access, Bitcoin meetups and global conferences are ripe with opportunities to meet potential mentors.

One surprising truth about mentorship is that its rewards are not as one-sided as we tend to think. The relationship is mutually beneficial. In the same way you, as a mentee, get to tap into your mentor's wealth of knowledge and experience, they also find it rewarding to share. Taking you under their tutelage gives them a chance to reflect on their past experiences and contribute to the growth of the next generation of investors. So, don't be surprised if you approach a highly admired veteran investor and they excitedly tell you, "Oh, I'm more than happy to share!"

If meeting seasoned investors in person is not feasible, you can still explore online mentorship programs within the Bitcoin community. These structured programs connect mentees with experienced investors and create an environment where learning and growth flourish.

But what if mentorship isn't your thing? Does that mean you can't learn from successful investors? Absolutely not. Thanks to the Internet, you have access to countless case studies detailing how seasoned Bitcoin investors have achieved success.

Take, for example, Michael Saylor, the Executive Chairman of MicroStrategy, whose bold investments have earned him a legendary reputation in the Bitcoin world. Saylor's approach showcases the value of strategic thinking and a long-term vision, which are qualities every successful investor needs. Even during Bitcoin's early days of skepticism, he recognized its potential as "digital gold," and as a hedge against inflation with immense growth opportunities.

To capitalize on this vision, Saylor employed a disciplined dollar-cost averaging strategy, which enabled his company to amass a significant Bitcoin portfolio. His success demonstrates the rewards of consistent and deliberate investing. Of course, his path wasn't without challenges, but instead of giving up, he used setbacks as opportunities to refine his strategies and strengthen his resolve. His story is a testament to the importance of conviction and adaptability in navigating the unpredictable crypto market.

When you take time to study examples like Saylor's, you are taking the position of their mentee to a large extent. You not only develop more than admiration but also acquire actionable insights. Through these stories, you will gain practical knowledge about the importance of perseverance during market volatility, the necessity of calculated risks, and the value of evolving strategies to fit changing circumstances.

So, either you choose to seek out a mentor or learn virtually from the stories of successful investors, the most important thing is that you do not navigate the Bitcoin journey alone. As a beginner, you need such experiences and lessons to grow into a confident and capable investor. So, don't be scared to take that first step of connecting and learning.

SHARING KNOWLEDGE AND CONTRIBUTING TO THE CRYPTO COMMUNITY

Despite the transformative advantages of mentorship, your quest to learn and grow should never end at absorbing the wisdom of those who have walked this path before you. True knowledge isn't just about taking. You need to give back too!

Of course, learning from experienced investors and mentors is game-changing, But there's something even more special about sharing what you have learned. It's like passing the baton in a relay race; every bit of insight you share helps move the whole community forward. And what happens when the community wins? You win too!

Have you heard of the saying "Knowledge shared is knowledge squared?" By sharing your knowledge of Bitcoin investing, you get to help others just as much as you reinforce your understanding. Explaining things forces you to think them through, and the questions you get from others can open your eyes to perspectives you hadn't considered. This back-and-forth makes the learning process richer for everyone involved.

Interestingly, taking this role of a mini coach can also help in building your reputation as a thoughtful and informed leader in the crypto space. With such a noble reputation comes the most unexpected but incredible opportunities like invitations to join exciting projects, meeting like-minded people, or just feeling good about contributing to a shared goal. In the Bitcoin space, every exchange of ideas adds to the collective intelligence that keeps the community thriving.

Now, you might be thinking, "I'm just a newbie in this game. What could I possibly have that could be beneficial?" The answer is simple—Whatever you have learned. If you like writing, try creating blog posts or articles to share your journey, concepts you found most confusing, or just Bitcoin investing trends that catch your eye. If you don't have a personal blog, you can share your writings on platforms like Medium or the available crypto forums. I promise you that as you become consistent, you will grow an audience of newbie investors just like you, who are hungry for knowledge.

Perhaps writing isn't your thing. As an alternative, you can organize and host webinars which allows for real-time discussions with other participants who may also have things to share. Today, we also have podcasts that let you share your story and connect with others in a more relaxed and conversational way. Go for it if you are more of a "casual chat" person.

Beyond these valuable benefits, you must understand that sharing is a responsibility just as it is an act of nobility. So, always take the time to verify your facts and ensure the information you share is accurate and trustworthy. This dedication boosts your credibility and helps you maintain the standard of trust and transparency that the Bitcoin community upholds.

DEVELOPING A GROWTH MINDSET FOR INVESTMENT SUCCESS

One of the toughest lessons I had to learn during my first year in Bitcoin trading was that things don't always go according to plan. By now, you know how unpredictable the Bitcoin market is, with the wildest mood swings hitting at the most unexpected times. While we've explored some of the best investment strategies—and even touched on the psychological and emotional tools to steady your nerves—there's one last secret weapon to tie it all together: a growth mindset.

In simple terms, a growth mindset is a way of thinking that views challenges and setbacks not as obstacles or failures, but as opportunities to grow and achieve success. Hear me out—you are bound to encounter challenges and failure in this journey. They are inevitable. But who knows what makes it better? A growth mindset!

While your colleagues are panicking and moaning in the face of their investment prices suddenly dropping, you will be the one calmly assessing the situation, ready to learn from it and pivot your strategy. Instead of seeing red, you will spot a chance to refine your approach, improve your decision-making, and ultimately come back stronger. Such is the power of a growth mindset! Trust me, there is none like it.

Now, how do you develop this extraordinary mindset? The ultimate key is to switch your focus from immediate results to long-term growth by constantly practicing some simple but highly advanced steps. The first is to embrace smaller manageable goals. You know those big dreams you have right now?—Break them into small steps. Every time you complete one step, no matter how minor it may seem, counts as a milestone. These small but timely victories will build your confidence and give you the momentum you need to keep moving forward.

Besides setting these incremental goals, you also need to become more introspective. So when setbacks come—and they will—try not to throw in the towel or panic. Instead, lean into them and reflect. Ask yourself, "What can I learn from this?" If you are into journaling, make time to pour out your thoughts on paper. The more you answer that one question, the easier it becomes to view every mistake, stumbling investment, or market dip as an opportunity to improve.

Flexibility and adaptability are also critical ingredients for building a growth mindset. Due to the volatility of Bitcoin and the entire crypto market, you will likely struggle with frustration if you stick rigidly to one plan. So, stay adaptable. If a particular strategy isn't working, don't be afraid to make small changes to it or try something completely new. Sometimes, this adaptability might require you to move out of your comfort zone like when you have to increase your risk tolerance or switch to a new trading strategy. If you genuinely know that it's the best move, please don't hesitate to do it. You also have to stay open to new investment opportunities especially those that allow you to capitalize on emerging trends and technologies.

Finally, you have to commit to lifelong learning. The most successful traders are those who continue to educate themselves whether through reading up on new trends, taking courses, or learning from the experiences of others. The more knowledge you acquire, the more confident you'll become in making decisions. So, never stop being a student of the market!

In the end, you should know that developing a growth mindset is far-fetched from avoiding mistakes or trying to predict the future. More than anything, it's about embracing every part of the process—the good, bad, and ugly—and staying open to change, So, be flexible and remember that a setback today could be the key to a breakthrough tomorrow!

BALANCING BITCOIN INVESTING WITH LIFE GOALS

In the introduction of this chapter, we mentioned that Bitcoin investing is only a part of "the bigger picture". That bigger picture is your life! The most successful investors are those who can align their Bitcoin investments with their personal values and life goals. Thus, beyond building profitable investments and growing your portfolio, you must ensure that your financial choices serve a greater purpose and contribute to the life you want to create.

When your investments are in sync with your bigger goals, they don't just exist in a vacuum. They improve your overall well-being and make your life fulfilling and balanced.

So, as you prepare to begin your investing journey, think of Bitcoin as a tool, not the ultimate goal. Of course, its growth potential is magnanimous. Still, it should fit well into your long-term aspirations, whether that means achieving financial independence, funding personal projects or even securing a comfortable retirement. By using the gains from your Bitcoin investments to fund these pursuits, you get to turn your financial success into meaningful life experiences.

To create this significant balance, you need to first clarify your priorities. So, ask yourself: What kind of life do I want to create? What values are most important to me? Once you've established what matters most, you can start aligning your Bitcoin investments with those aspirations. For instance, if traveling more or pursuing further education is your life goal, you can prioritize investments that help you achieve those dreams, rather than focusing solely on short-term profits or portfolio numbers.

Now that your goals are clear, it's time to integrate Bitcoin investing into your life with balance. You can do so by setting boundaries. So, schedule dedicated time for researching and managing your investments. Perhaps a few hours each week to track market trends, analyze your portfolio's performance, and make necessary adjustments. Since it is so easy to get caught up in the market excitement, these boundaries will ensure that you do not let your investments take over or disrupt your personal life. With this healthy balance, you can maintain a lifestyle that accommodates both your financial planning and personal pursuits,

To sustain your balance, you have to conduct consistent and mindful reviews. So, assess your investments regularly and see how they match your goals. If needed, you can make adjustments or get advice from financial experts to guide you. The most important thing is you stay connected to your goals, with your financial decisions fitting perfectly with the bigger picture!

Looking at the four sections we've covered in this chapter, it's clear that success in Bitcoin investing requires a balance of collaboration and personal growth. Building a support system through networking and mentorship ensures you have access to shared knowledge, diverse perspectives, and emotional backing during market highs and lows. At the same time, personal growth, which is fueled by your growth mindset, clear life goals, and mindful investment practices, empowers you to navigate Bitcoin challenges confidently and make financial decisions that align with your values.

Both sides are crucial for your long-term success, not just in Bitcoin investing, but in your overall financial journey. So, try your best to create that balance! And remember, that it's not just about the numbers but also the life you want to create!

FUTURE-PROOFING YOUR BITCOIN INVESTMENTS

If we had the time to look through the historical records of Bitcoin and other cryptocurrencies, we would see loud and clear that change is the only constant in this space. For most of this book, we have emphasized the wild price spikes that the Bitcoin market continuously experiences. But more than that, this space has witnessed technology advancements, regulatory changes, and shifting investor dynamics that have completely changed the game from what it used to be in its early days.

Now, what has this preamble got to do with you? Everything! To be a successful investor, you must understand that nothing about the Bitcoin market will last forever. Hence, you have to anticipate what's coming next and match your investment strategies with where the future is heading.

This finale is your guide to doing exactly that! We will be discussing sustainable and ethical Bitcoin strategies, the growing influence of big institutions in crypto, and why staying curious about blockchain innovations could be your smartest move yet.

Now, if you are ready to learn how to keep your hard-earned investments future-ready, take my hand, and let's take the last turn of this knowledge-seeking adventure!

SUSTAINABLE AND ETHICAL INVESTING IN BITCOIN

While deconstructing the science behind Bitcoin's blockchain technology, we explored how mining works and its relevance to quick and efficient transactions. However, we also emphasized it is an energy-intensive process that requires substantial computational power and consumes vast amounts of electricity. Remember that? Well, that explanation was just putting it mildly. Research studies have shown that Bitcoin's energy usage is often compared to that of an entire country. That's quite staggering, right? And to make matters worse, much of this energy comes from non-renewable sources which further fuel the global carbon footprint.

As you can imagine, Bitcoin's environmental impact is becoming harder to overlook. But the positive side is that some Bitcoin companies are stepping up and tapping into renewable energy sources like wind, solar, and hydropower to power their mining operations. These innovative eco-friendly approaches are slowly but surely helping to create a more sustainable path for Bitcoin's future.

But the drive for sustainability in the Bitcoin space should not be one-sided. As an investor, you have the ethical responsibility to support mining companies that prioritize ethical and transparent practices like clearly communicating energy sources and impacts. You can also choose to back initiatives that demonstrate a commitment to reducing environmental harm. Every project you back is a vote for the ethically responsible crypto ecosystem you want to see.

To know if the projects you are investing in are truly sustainable, you can assess them using the ESG (Environmental, Social, Governance) metrics. These metrics provide a structured way to evaluate the sustainability and ethical practices of cryptocurrency projects by considering factors like environmental impact, social responsibility, and governance structures. You can also look out for green certifications and audits, as they are reliable benchmarks for identifying projects that meet high sustainability standards.

If you are willing to commit even further to making a difference, you might want to join and participate actively in sustainability-focused crypto initiatives like the Project "Green" by Ethereum and The Carbon Credit Blockchain Project. Beyond driving sustainability, these projects address global challenges, like improving supply chain transparency or promoting financial inclusion. That's killing two birds with one! You get to enhance the social and environmental impact of your investments while also increasing the funds in your wallet!

THE IMPACT OF INSTITUTIONAL INVESTMENTS IN CRYPTOCURRENCY

Back in Chapter Two, we touched on the emerging developments in cryptocurrency and pointed out the growing presence of institutional investors as a major game-changer. They are truly shaking things up in the crypto space!

Their entry into the scene over the last few years has brought in a considerable amount of liquidity (money) which is gradually calming the infamous mood swings of the Bitcoin market. Yes, I mean those dramatic price drops and spikes! With Bitcoin now looking a lot less like a rollercoaster and more like a smooth cruise, more conservative investors are joining the ship.

This increasing participation of reputable institutions is also serving as a powerful endorsement to cement Bitcoin's status as a legitimate asset. Companies like MicroStrategy and Tesla were the first to join the Bitcoin bandwagon and their moves turned heads and changed how corporate treasuries work. Then, big financial names like Fidelity and Grayscale came and officially solidified that Bitcoin now belonged in the big leagues. With these high-standard endorsements, it's no surprise that more people—including you, perhaps—are starting to view Bitcoin investing as a serious opportunity.

But then, what could be driving these large-scale investors to explore Bitcoin? Well for one, diversification! Bitcoin offers a unique asset that behaves differently than traditional stocks and bonds. Let's not forget the protection against economic uncertainties and inflation! With central banks calling the shots and world politics getting more complicated, Bitcoin offers these big institutional players a refreshing alternative that comprises greater control over their assets and more importantly, higher returns!

Now, what does all this mean for regular investors like you and me? Well, it's a mixed reality. On the one hand, institutional involvement has brought us innovative financial products like Exchange-Traded Funds (ETFs), which makes it easier than ever to add Bitcoin to your investment lineup, notwithstanding whether it's your retirement or other cryptocurrency accounts.

On the other hand, the presence of institutional investors is creating more competition for market influence and price stability. Since they wield significant financial power, their actions can sway market trends and pricing. So, as a retail investor, your key to staying ahead of the game is to be constantly updated about the strategies or policies introduced by these large-scale investors.

Based on the pros and cons we've just explored, do you think institutional investments have been a blessing or a curse for Bitcoin? It's not a straightforward answer, is it? If you ask me, I'd say it's a bit of both. On one side, they have brought much-needed stability, legitimacy, and wider adoption to the crypto space. Yet, their dominance can feel a bit like the cool kids taking over the playground and leaving retail investors to conquer new challenges.

Notwithstanding, you will agree that the benefits outweigh the disadvantages. How? With more visibility and acceptance, Bitcoin's future as a mainstream asset becomes brighter. And the more credible Bitcoin becomes, the more opportunities it creates for all of us, whether we're trading, holding, or just watching from the sidelines. That's a win!

EMBRACING TECHNOLOGICAL INNOVATIONS IN BLOCKCHAIN

When we first analyzed the dynamics of blockchain technology in Chapter One, you were probably in awe of its fascinating and transformative capabilities. Trust me, I felt the same, too! But apparently, the masterminds behind blockchain weren't as easily impressed. In recent years, they have pushed the boundaries of what this technology can achieve by producing advancements that are not only improving Bitcoin's functionality but also redefining how we interact with digital assets.

One such game-changing upgrade is Layer 2 solutions like the Lightning Network, which addresses scalability issues inherent in Bitcoin's original design. The Lightning Network enables faster and cheaper transactions by processing them off-chain before allowing them to settle on the blockchain. The most incredible part of this innovation is that it brings us one step closer to using Bitcoin for everyday purchases. Can you imagine what it will be like to buy a cup of coffee using Bitcoin? Probably not! But the development of the Lightning Network assures us that it's coming soon!

Another recent breakthrough is the rise of cross-chain solutions, which are simply the "translators" of the blockchain world. These information exchange protocols allow different blockchain networks to communicate and share data seamlessly. So unlike the first few years of Bitcoin's investments, investors like you and I can now trade assets directly between blockchains or by using "wrapped" versions of Bitcoin on other networks. So simply put, the development of these cross-chain solutions has helped in creating a more connected and cooperative digital world where blockchains of different digital assets work together smoothly.

Now, remember smart contract technology from Chapter Two? While we identified it then as the exceptional powerhouse behind Ethereum, this network is now being integrated into Bitcoin thanks to advancements like Taproot and Schnorr signatures. With this integration, the Bitcoin network is slowly enjoying the luxury of automated and trustless transactions, where there is no need for intermediaries like miners.

At this point, you will agree that each of the three technological developments we discussed in this chapter has powerful implications for the Bitcoin world. As such, we, as investors, must engage proactively with them.

To get more insights about these developments, you can join blockchain development communities or attend conferences focused specifically on blockchain advancements. These platforms allow you to stay updated on the latest trends, collaborate with like-minded individuals, and even contribute to ongoing projects. In short, they can help in elevating your success, as a Bitcoin investor!

CONCLUSION

Have you ever had a dream so big yet so far from your current reality that it felt almost impossible to achieve? For me, I've had two. The first was achieving financial freedom, and Bitcoin investing made that dream a reality. The second was writing this book.

For years, I stalled and told myself, *"It's not the right time."* But eventually, that time came, and here we are at the finish line. I use "we" because this journey isn't just mine. It's ours. You, the reader, are the real champion. By picking up this book, you took the bold step of transforming your financial future and for that, you deserve to be celebrated.

So, let's take a moment to appreciate how far you and I have come. Together, we began by exploring the foundational principles of Bitcoin, from its revolutionary origins to its undeniable impact on decentralized finance. Then, we took a long walk through the incredible mechanics of blockchain and followed the flow of Bitcoin transactions like detectives uncovering clues. We even took a detour to meet Bitcoin's fascinating cousins, the Altcoins where we learned how they add color and variety to the cryptocurrency world.

With that solid foundation laid, we jumped headfirst into the practical stuff of buying Bitcoins and trading them like a pro. We learned how to navigate the market, make smart decisions, and build investments that could grow into something spectacular. Then came the strategy! We unlocked game-changing investing strategies, risk management tips, and the steps to creating a diversified cryptocurrency portfolio.

Of course, we couldn't just stay technical the entire time. We had to get personal, didn't we? We dug into the psychological and emotional side of investing—those moments of doubt, excitement, and sometimes panic. Together, we learned how to keep our cool, think strategically, and embrace the market volatility as part of the journey.

Finally, we wrapped things up by looking ahead into the future. We explored the role of ethical investing and technological innovations and how they continue to shape the future of Bitcoin and cryptocurrency.

You would agree that we had quite the adventure! But more than learning the ins and outs of Bitcoin, this journey has been about discovering the power within yourself to take control of your financial future. And you stood up to the task! You prove that you're willing to learn, grow, and take risks to create a better life for yourself and those you love. That's the one true quality of a champion and I cannot be more proud to have been your guide.

With the knowledge and strategies you've gained through the nine chapters of this book, I know that you are ready to leverage the power of Bitcoin investing to shape your financial destiny and ignite the most exciting transformation of your life.

So, more than anything, I want you to feel empowered as you move forward. Of course, Bitcoin is a life-changing asset but the real magic lies in what you do with it. Your dreams, values, and goals are what make this journey worthwhile. Whether it's building a legacy for your family, funding your passions, or simply having the freedom to live life on your terms, remember that your investments are a means to a greater end.

I also want you to know that you're not alone in this journey. My mission has always been to help individuals like you achieve financial freedom, and that commitment doesn't end here. I encourage you to reach out with your questions, share your experiences, and seek guidance whenever you need it. I wholeheartedly promise that I will be there to answer.

I could go on and on, but it's best I let you go so that you can begin this next chapter of your life where you take everything you've learned and turn your dreams into reality. Remember that this journey is yours to own. While the pages of this book may end here, your story of growth is just beginning.

So, slowly take a deep breath. Trust in your newfound knowledge, and step boldly into your future. You have everything it takes to succeed, and Bitcoin and all its possibilities are waiting for you to claim them. And as you do, know that I'm cheering for you every step of the way. Here's to your continued growth, empowerment, and prosperity in the cryptocurrency space.

LEAVE A 1-CLICK REVIEW

I would be incredibly thankful if you take just 60-seconds to write a brief review on Amazon, even if it's just a few sentences!

https://www.champlinks.com/sl/Bitcoin-Paperback-Review/

ABOUT THE AUTHOR

Conrad Presley is uniquely equipped to analyze and discuss the deep-rooted factors that drive ongoing conflicts, drawing on his academic background in psychology, sociology, and finance.

As the owner of multiple thriving businesses, he takes great pleasure in mentoring aspiring entrepreneurs and believes that by helping others succeed, we can all contribute to making the world a better place.

In addition to his expertise in finance, Conrad is also well-versed in cryptocurrency and blockchain technology, having navigated the ever-evolving world of digital finance for years. As a passionate advocate for financial empowerment, he has a gift for simplifying complex concepts and making them accessible to readers of all levels.

This book is a testament to his desire to guide readers through the intricacies of digital currencies, empowering them to make informed decisions and harness the power of blockchain to shape their financial future. But Conrad's impact goes beyond the finance domain. He serves as a bridge between psychology, sociology, and business, offering insightful and impactful strategies for personal growth and professional success. Through his work, he continues to inspire individuals and organizations to reach their full potential and make a positive impact in the world.

REFERENCES

Abbas, S.A. (2023). The Rise of Altcoins: Exploring Beyond Bitcoin in the Crypto Universe. Retrieved From https://medium.com/@zee.associates001/the-rise-of-Altcoins-exploring-beyond-bitcoin-in-the-crypto-universe-869baf519583

Arif, A.. (2024). Decentralized Finance (DeFi) and Its Impact on Traditional Finance. Retrieved from https://papers.ssrn.com/sol3/papers.cfm?abstract_id=4942313

Bajpai, P. (2024). Countries Where Bitcoin Is Legal and Illegal. Retrieved from https://www.investopedia.com/articles/forex/041515/countries-where-bitcoin-legal-illegal.asp

Bitpay. 2024). HODL: What Does It Mean & How Did It Start? Retrieved from https://bitpay.com/blog/origins-of-hodl-in-crypto

Daly, L. (2024). How to Create a Well-Balanced Crypto Portfolio. Retrieved from https://www.fool.com/investing/stock-market/market-sectors/financials/cryptocurrency-stocks/crypto-portfolio

Draper, A. (2024). 15+ Best DeFi Wallets to Store Your Crypto in 2024. Retrieved from https://www.business2community.com/cryptocurrency/best-defi-wallets?gad_source=1&gclid=CjwKCAiA65m7BhAwEiwAAgu4JCA_sPGAyWJa3Ibfq5aPx_dn2oNuDH0nBim307nNSr1SDC-r1T_JchoCa5EQAvD_BwE

Goncalo de Vasconcelos. (2018). ICOs: The Good, The Bad, and The Future. Retrieved from https://www.forbes.com/sites/goncalodevasconcelos/2018/05/31/icos-the-good-the-bad-and-the-ugly/

Guneet, K (2024). Crypto Charts 101: How to Read Cryptocurrency Charts. Retrieved from https://cointelegraph.com/learn/articles/crypto-charts-101-how-to-read-cryptocurrency-charts

Hayes, A. (2024). How to Buy Bitcoin. Retrieved from https://www.investopedia.com/articles/investing/082914/basics-buying-and-investing-bitcoin.asp

Jones, P. (2024).Kaur, G. (2023). What is a Phishing Attack in Crypto, and How to Prevent It? Retrieved from https://cointelegraph.com/learn/articles/what-is-a-phishing-attack-in-crypto-and-how-to-prevent-it

Legge, M. (2024). 10 Best Crypto Trading Bots December 2024 | Expert Review. Retrieved from https://koinly.io/blog/best-crypto-trading-bots

Lielacher, A. (2024). Best Crypto Exchanges and Apps for December 2024 Retrieved from https://www.investopedia.com/best-crypto-exchanges-5071855

Majaski, C. (2024). Day Trading vs. Swing Trading: What's the Difference? Retrieved from https://www.investopedia.com/articles/active-trading/052815/pros-cons-day-trading-vs-swing-trading.asp

One Trading (2023). 10 Popular Altcoins to Watch in 2023. Retrieved from https://onetrading.com/blogs/10-popular-Altcoins-to-watch-in-2023 .

One Trading. (2023). How to Choose the Best Crypto Exchange: 10 Essential Tips. Retrieved from https://onetrading.com/blogs/10-essential-tips-for-choosing-the-best-crypto-exchange

Parkin, D. (2024).15 years of disruption and innovation — and why this will continue. Retrieved from https://cryptotech.com/advancements

Reiff, N. (2024). What's the Environmental Impact of Cryptocurrency? Retrieved from https://www.investopedia.com/tech/whats-environmental-impact-cryptocurrency/

River Learn. (2023). How Do Bitcoin Transactions Work? Retrieved from https://river.com/learn/how-does-a-bitcoin-transaction-work/

Rodriguez, G..O. (2024). 11 Best Crypto Wallets of December 2024. Retrieved from https://money.com/best-crypto-wallets/

Saleem, S. Z. (2018). The 2008 Global Meltdown and the Birth of Bitcoin. Retrieved from https://www.livemint.com/Money/YTYMYUD7dytGK5PGSpdRTN/The-2008-global-meltdown-and-the-birth-of-Bitcoin.html

Stanford Engineering Center for Global & Online Education. (2020). How Does Blockchain Work? Retrieved from https://online.stanford.edu/how-does-blockchain-work

The Economic Times. (2024). From skepticism to acceptance: How institutions are embracing cryptocurrencies. Retrieved from https://www.-google.com/amp/s/m.economictimes.com/markets/cryptocurrency/from-skepticism-to-acceptance-how-institutions-are-embracing-cryptocurrencies/amp_articleshow/114071521.cms

The Investopedia Team. (2023). Decentralized Applications (dApps): Definition, Uses, Pros and Cons. Retrieved from https://www.investopedia.com/terms/d/decentralized-applications-dapps.asp

The Investopedia Team. (2024). What Is Bitcoin Mining? How to Get Started. Retrieved from https://www.investopedia.com/terms/b/bitcoin-mining.asp

Walker, G. (2023). An Introduction to Bitcoin DeFi. Retrieved from https://

trustmachines.co/learn/bitcoin-decentralized-finance-defi/#:~:text=Decentralized%20platforms%20have%20ways%20to,for%20trading%20or%20arbitrage%20purposes

White, K. (2023). How to Safeguard Your Bitcoin Assets. Retrieved from https://safeguardbitcoin.com

Wilson, K. (2024). US ICO Regulations - Complete Guide. Retrieved from https://sdlccorp.com/post/us-ico-regulations-complete-guide/

Made in the USA
Monee, IL
04 November 2026

67382834R10075